MARKETING TO WIN

MARKETING TO WIN

Strategies for Building Competitive Advantage in Service Industries

---

Frank K. Sonnenberg

National Director of Marketing
Management Consulting
Ernst & Young

 HarperBusiness

A Division of HarperCollins*Publishers*

International Standard Book Number: 0-88730-420-6

Library of Congress Catalog Card Number 90-4178

Printed in the United States of America

Library of Congress Cataloging-in-Publication Data

Sonnenberg, Frank K.
    Marketing to win / by Frank K. Sonnenberg.
        p. cm.
    Includes bibliographical references.
    ISBN 0-88730-420-6
    1. Marketing.   2. Customer service.   I. Title.
HF5415.S6932   1990
658.8—dc20   90-4178
                                                   CIP

91 92 93 CCHC 9 8 7 6 5 4 3 2

*To my wife, Caron,
and my daughters, Cathy and Kristy,
who make everything worthwhile.*

Contents

Acknowledgments

This book represents the contributions of many people to whom I am most grateful.

First, I would like to thank all the people who took the time to review early drafts of this book and provide me with their valuable insights: Marti Brink, Ed Rosen, Mark Sandberg, Skip Tolette, Tammy Mitchell, Joe Fiore, Ed Shulman, David Tierno, Bob LaVine, Michael Sullivan, Ann Marie Lombardi, Karen Kichline Ruef, Pat Wagner, Joe Dattoli, Andy Corn, Richard Shapiro, Lisa Galjanic, Herb Natter, Bob Drew, Pat Pollino, and Virginia Smith and Mark Greenberg of Harper & Row.

I would like to thank Nancy Pratt and *The Journal of Business Strategy* for providing me with the initial forum in which to express the ideas and concepts upon which this book was conceived.

Special mention should be made to the individuals who collaborated with me in preparing the articles upon which the following chapters are based: Chapter 2, David Tierno; Chapter 3, Michael Graupner; Chapter 4, Tammy Mitchell; and Chapter 8, Richard Sasanow.

Thanks also to my friends and colleagues at Ernst & Young, far too numerous to list here, whose encouragement and insight are reflected in this book.

Next, I'd like to offer special thanks to three people:

To Mark Sandberg, associate dean of the School of Business Administration at Rider College (to which the proceeds of this book are being contributed). Mark has devoted his life to the personal and professional development of his students. He is such a giving person that he takes more pleasure from his contributions to the successes of others than from his own successes. Through the DAARSTOC leadership development program that he founded and through his dedication, personal guidance, and wisdom, he has touched numerous lives and is the force behind countless success stories. If this country is to remain great, we must invest in the future leaders of America; to do so, we will need more educators like Mark.

To David Tierno. If not for Dave, this book would never have been written. I want to thank him for his encouragement, his unwavering support, his thoughtful observations, and his valuable feedback. Some people learn about leadership through trial and error, some by reading books, and others from careful observation. Dave, thank you for serving as a personal role model that anyone would be proud to have.

To Beverly Goldberg. Behind every Olympian is the coach who should equally share in the moment of victory. I want to thank her for her gifted writing; for the weekend discussions and early morning conversations; for her patience, stamina, persistence, and dedication; but most of all, for caring about this book as if it were her own.

Last but not least, I'd like to thank my family. To my mother and father, for instilling in me the values that are so much a part of this book. To my wife, Caron, who lived every word with me. She provided encouragement, patience, and understanding when this book kept me from her side, and she herself devoted hours to it, reviewing and offering keen insights into the manuscript.

Thank you all.

Today, more than ever, organizations must execute and imple-ment—not just talk about the need to provide more quality and service. Marketing to Win *clearly lays out the practical direction for making the 1990s the decade of the customer.*
—Buck Rodgers, former worldwide vice president, Marketing, IBM Corporation.

MARKETING TO WIN

1

Introduction: Survival of the Fittest

Open your eyes—the world around you is changing at an unprecedented rate. The globalization of products and services and the deregulation of markets are altering the very nature of competition. Reports show that there have been over 90,000 mergers and acquisitions since 1986. Rapidly changing technology is reducing the product life cycle, affecting the way products and services are developed and delivered; at the same time, consumers have become more sophisticated and more demanding.

Well folks, you are at a crossroad. Either recognize these dramatic changes and adapt or forget about competing successfully in the new marketing era. To pursue the latter course, close your eyes, put on your blinders, and announce, "It may happen to them, but never me." In other words, adopt a philosophy of business as usual.

I'm saying that the leaders of today may not be the leaders of tomorrow. I'm saying that those proud of their winging it, flip-a-coin, shoot-from-the-hip mentality will not succeed in this new environment. I'm saying that the quick-fix, program-of-the-month, Band-Aid approach to marketing will no longer compensate for inadequacies. I'm saying that organizational politics such as backstabbing, maneuvering, infighting, or promoting one's own interests will prove a catalyst—not for personal success, but for an organization's demise.

The bottom line is that if you don't change now, you may as

well start filling your scrapbook with memories of today. It is unlikely you will have much to show for tomorrow.

What does it take not only to survive but to thrive in this competitive environment? It starts with seven basic philosophies.

Seven Guideposts to Success

Marketing Is More Than Common Sense—There Is a Right Way

When your competitors know more than you do, you are at a disadvantage.*

Did you know that visuals used during presentations make you look more professional and make what you are saying seem far more persuasive, credible, and interesting? Did you know that the probability of an audience reaching consensus is 79 percent with visuals and 58 percent without them? Did you know that visuals using words printed in capital letters are harder to read than ones in uppercase and lowercase letters (in fact, studies have shown that visuals in uppercase and lowercase are between 13 and 14 percent faster to read, as well as more legible and pleasant to read, and that reading rates are slowed by 8 to 11 percent when you mix italic, roman, and boldface type)?

Do you know how important quality service is to your organization? In a recent survey of 2,374 customers, more than 40 percent listed poor service as the number one reason for switching to the competition, while only 8 percent listed price. Did you know that the average person who has been burned by an organization tells nine to ten colleagues about that experience, and that 13 percent of dissatisfied customers spread the bad news to more than 20 people? Moreover, studies have shown that companies rated highly by their clients for service can charge close to 9 percent more than those rated poorly.

How effectively do you communicate? Did you know that

*The facts listed in this chapter are elaborated on and sources for them given in the book.

research shows that we spend seven out of every ten minutes that we are awake communicating, and that communication time is devoted 9 percent to writing, 16 percent to reading, 30 percent to speaking, and 45 percent to listening? And did you know that immediately after hearing someone speak, most people remember only about half of what was said, no matter how carefully they were listening? Furthermore, research shows that two months later, the average listener will remember only about 25 percent of what was said. The communication problem proves even worse when examining internal communications in an organization. Research shows that understanding falls off considerably as communication flows downward. In the case of communicating through five levels of an organization, only 20 percent of a message finally gets through to workers.

When actively developing new services, creating promotional materials, generating new business leads, managing and improving sales performance, enhancing presentation skills, maintaining and increasing client relationships, implementing cross-selling programs, and organizing internally to support the marketing and sales effort, facts are always preferred to guesses, even best guesses.

Ready-Fire-Aim Misses Targets

How many times have you heard people say, "We don't have the time to plan, our competitors are breathing down our backs" or "Let's get something out there quickly, then once the business comes in we'll develop a strategy and do it the right way"?

The reality is that if you operate without a plan, without a carefully developed strategy, business rarely comes in. Everyone runs around working at cross-purposes, duplicating the efforts of others, making false starts, and spending a great deal of time putting out fires. What is even more unfortunate about this mind-set is that the same process is then repeated time and time again.

Tactics before strategy is bad business. The probability of achieving success increases the closer you come to reaching a balance between too little and too much planning. As one consultant once put it, "If you spend too much time warming up, you'll miss the race; if you don't warm up at all, you may never finish."

Strategic thinking must precede and permeate every business move. It is why building lasting relationships with clients requires more than taking people out to an expensive lunch or to a baseball game on Saturday, and more than just a friendly telephone call every two weeks. Furthermore, it is why treating networking as a game of business bumper cars, showing up at meetings two minutes before they start, never making a contribution, failing to expend the time needed to get to know people on a personal level, and then frantically passing out your business cards to everyone you see are a waste of everyone's time.

Having a clear purpose—what are you trying to achieve and how do you plan to get there—may sound obvious, yet lack of attention to this fundamental precept is a very common error. People frantically run around making themselves feel good by keeping busy; what they forget is that there is a big difference between motion and movement. The former is energy expended without an objective; the latter consists of methodically moving from point A to point B. A clear goal also allows members of an organization to work together toward a common end instead of pursuing independent goals.

A Means or an End

A ready-fire-aim philosophy is a major cause of the next fundamental business error—not being able to distinguish whether an activity or program is a means to an end or an end in itself.

Besides guiding everyone in the right direction, a clear purpose, established before beginning any marketing activity, serves as a benchmark against which the quality of the marketing effort and the magnitude of its achievement can be measured. Without it, people get caught up in irrelevant details or blind alleys that result in waste, if not downright failure.

For example:

- Plans are often measured by newness, bulk, complexity, or adherence to a prescribed format rather than by the strategies contained within them.

- Direct mail programs, trade shows, seminars, and other lead-generating activities are evaluated in terms of the number of leads received rather than the quality of the leads or the amount of business generated as a result of proper follow-up.
- Advertisements are measured in terms of their creativity or the awards they win rather than for their ability to generate awareness or increase revenues for the organization.

Furthermore, company management often focuses its efforts on the development, production, and dissemination of internal communication as ends in themselves rather than as means to an end. All too often a great deal of time is lost nit-picking words rather than ensuring that all of the communication activities are consistent in meaning and bring about a desired behavior. In other words, a newsletter is judged by its appearance and a video by how attractive the executive looks on television—no one stops to judge how well either communicates its message to the audience or if the message achieves its initial objective.

Blocking and Tackling

As Vince Lombardi noted, in football you don't win or lose based on grand strategies, but by taking care of the basics, by making the tackle or block. The same concept applies to business. That is why, during the strategic planning process, one should not only set goals and objectives but also tactics for accomplishing them. The reason why so many strategic plans fail is that they are poorly executed. Plans must be properly implemented, with adequate attention given to small details; there must be continuous monitoring and updating. In other words, proper execution of a strategy requires giving the same concern, the same focus, to each transaction that you give to the grand overall design.

As an example, in developing a direct mail campaign, many people focus their efforts solely on the creative portion of the program and treat the development of the mailing list as an afterthought. The reality is that no matter how well a message is developed, it is worthless if it is delivered to the wrong audience.

Experts claim that half of the effort put into a direct mail campaign should be on list development.

Rifle Versus Shotgun Marketing

Military strategy teaches the tactics of mass—the concentration of superior resources where they are most critical. In marketing, examples of such strategies include the concentration of resources on two or three services instead of many, targeting specific industries to develop a real expertise or niche, or selecting key geographical locations where you can marshal superior manpower.

Seen in this light, achieving competitive advantage means setting priorities and making choices. It means that to get results in the marketplace, your focus must be on positioning your firm and differentiating your services from the competition. You cannot try to be all things to all people; that approach gives you no competitive advantage whatsoever. Indeed, it is a recipe for poor performance and outright failure.

In an example of shotgun marketing, many companies and individuals spend a great deal of time searching for new clients, ignoring the opportunities that can be found in their own backyards. For example, when 20 percent of your clients are responsible for 80 percent of your business, those clients warrant special attention. When you have a client list like that, you must be careful not to devote too much of your effort to finding new clients. Instead, you should concentrate on servicing existing accounts, nurturing relationships, and finding new opportunities to expand your business relationships. A second approach is to focus attention on a few nonclients that provide real potential, narrowing your broad marketing effort to focus on those few potential accounts and then starting to build ongoing relationships with them.

This concept also applies to marketing communications where using mass-marketing techniques (that is, selling to broad groups) is analogous to air-conditioning an entire building in order to keep its only two occupied units cool. It works, but it may be inefficient. In contrast, direct mail, for example, targets the right audience with a message aimed directly at its needs.

Viewing Clients as Long-term Assets

Do you view your business relationships in terms of the one transaction you are about to make or in terms of the potential business that your firm could receive if you properly manage those relationships over the years? The way you answer that question will have an impact on every policy decision that your organization makes.

Short-term relationships are built on the one-shot deal; long-term relationships are built on a solid foundation of understanding a client's organization and recognizing its ongoing needs. In long-term relationships, you no longer play only a selling role but have shifted to an advisory role, providing real value to the buyer. Instead of continually searching for new prospects in many companies, you work at building ongoing relationships with a few.

This is a change from a hit-and-run philosophy to that of building for the future. With this approach you assume that at some point you will get paid back for all your efforts on behalf of a client. The return may be in word-of-mouth referral or in additional business, but it will happen.

Continuous Improvement: One Step Backward, Two Forward

There are two very important lessons about making mistakes. The first I learned early in life. It is that everyone makes mistakes, but if I'm smart enough to learn from those mistakes, I won't make them again. Later, I learned that I don't necessarily have to make every mistake in the world myself in order to learn: I can learn by observing the mistakes and misfortunes of others.

A philosophy emphasizing continuous improvement should be instilled in all employees. For example, every time you make a sales call or deliver a presentation, you should make it a habit to ask yourself, "If I had the opportunity to make the call again, what would I do differently?" or "How could I make it more effective next time?" And every time a client is lost or a proposal is rejected, you should conduct a postmortem—not to find fault, but to see how the situation could be avoided in the future.

Complaints should be welcome and viewed as an opportunity to improve policies and procedures. In fact, problem resolution offers a means of making customers aware of your concern about them.

Another road to continuous improvement—and a way to gauge your performance—is the account review. This meeting—whether quarterly, semiannual, or annual—between the buyer and seller of services allows both parties a chance to review perspectives. What are the client's objectives? Their accomplishments? What are the problems and obstacles preventing future success? Such candid discussions can bring parties closer together and contribute to a lasting relationship.

Marketing to Win: Ingredients of Success

There are six vital components of an effective marketing organization.

Leadership

Tomorrow's leaders must do more than manage numbers and be the caretakers of the day-to-day business. Their job is not pressuring employees for immediate results but articulating a vision, enlisting support and involvement for a common cause, and cementing bonds between people—pulling rather than pushing toward a goal. Leaders must motivate, help people grow and develop personally and professionally, and inspire them to achieve their maximum potential. And they must see that their organization has a clear mission, that its goals are clearly defined, and that employees know what roles they are expected to play and what the rewards of playing the roles successfully will be. Without such leadership, the organization will fail.

Communication

Communication is the vehicle leaders use to focus and direct their employees. Leaders must find a way to communicate company values and beliefs, or, over time, the meaning of those beliefs and values are lost. Leaders also communicate the type of organization they are running through their choice of the individuals they surround themselves with, the way they set their priorities, the consistency of their actions and words, the way they promote people, and the way they introduce new people into the organization.

The multifaceted nature of corporate communications means that leaders must ensure that all communications, both verbal and nonverbal, are consistent in meaning and reinforce one another. Everything is important, from bulletin boards to company T-shirts, from meeting formats to the size and location of offices, from office hours to access to executives, from holiday parties to retirement dinners.

But no matter how good communications are, remember that different people in an audience (whether internal or external) hear messages in different ways because they have different viewpoints, backgrounds, personal interests, education, experiences, and are in different levels within an organization. Thus, it is important to direct messages to different audiences in clear and precise terms, always addressing the needs of others in terms that are meaningful to them rather than to ourselves.

Individuality Versus Teamwork

People can maintain their individuality and still be good team members. Being part of a team does not mean that you have to be a yes person, forced into surrendering new and innovative ideas, afraid to fight for the changes that will make an organization great.

In some organizations, management makes it clear that employees are expected to do things a certain way—or else. What these organizations lose is the creative, dynamic, innovative spirit that is created when people get fired up for a cause. They do not understand that a team is created by blending the best of what every member has to offer to create a synergistic effect, working toward the betterment of the whole rather than of the individual. Teamwork is not setting rigid parameters that stifle individuality, making everyone walk in lockstep.

Coordination

Policies and procedures should not be developed for the convenience of the organization or its employees but for their overall impact on client service. There must be coordination between offices, divisions, functional areas, and geographic locations to see that clients are properly served. Clients will develop an unfavorable image of an organization if they are called upon three times a week by three different representatives of the same organization. Clients often become alienated if they are improperly billed because sales and administration haven't communicated, if they ask about a service an employee has yet to hear about from headquarters, and if they are bombarded with conflicting messages from various service groups within the organization. Avoiding these problems takes proper internal communication and coordination, and encouragement from management.

Many organizations believe that their image is based solely on the satisfactory delivery of a product or service. This is hardly the case. Clients develop an impression both before and after a sale is made. All the details, no matter how insignificant they seem, must be coordinated at every level. For example, a company is judged by such diverse factors as the way phone calls are answered, the impression its lobby gives, whether bills are properly prepared, the quality of product literature, and an employee's ability to answer an on-the-spot question. All the signals that a company sends should be coordinated to reflect a focused and consistent image.

Information Systems

In past years, information technology was primarily used to improve overall efficiency and back-office operations. Instead of performing a manual task, it seemed more productive to automate it. Today, however, more and more companies are using information technology to provide better service to clients, to decrease time to market, to gain access to better information necessary for making important business decisions—all of which help them achieve a competitive advantage.

Instant, accurate information is no longer a luxury. It is vital in today's competitive marketplace. A corporation has to know all there is about its clients and their buying patterns, down to such details as when and why they buy, what services the company has sold to them in the past, and what impact a price change or new service will have on them.

Integration

Integration, which is going to be a key marketing term in the 1990s, takes many forms. For example, there must be integration between business strategy and technology. Today, a gap exists between executives involved in determining key business strategies for their organizations and technologists responsible for developing the systems to drive and/or support those strategies. The walls between these groups must be torn down.

An organization must also be integrated to ensure that it presents a unified image externally. Many firms are organized into separate profit centers. They market their services to clients as though they represent completely different companies when, in fact, from the perspective of clients looking in, they represent one firm. An organization that competes for the same audiences rather than working together in a coordinated fashion appears disorganized, with its key message getting lost in the clutter. Successful companies will speak to clients as one organization.

Integration of various departments within an organization is also critical to companywide problems. All too often management believes that a brochure or a new compensation program or a single training seminar alone will magically make problems disappear. This piecemeal approach will never yield the proper results. What management fails to realize is that when addressing the cross-selling challenge, for example, no matter how appealing a reward may be, without proper training employees may not be able to describe accurately the services they're being asked to sell. Without information systems, they won't have timely information to service clients, and without marketing support, it may be difficult to get the word out to existing clients. Thus, marketing, training, information, and reward systems must be integrated to ensure that cross-selling takes place.

Finally, communications materials need to be integrated so that all forms of corporate communications are targeted and focused; the strategy, message, and medium chosen must all work together to achieve specific goals.

Becoming a Winner

There is a rhythm and logic to the marketing cycle. The first step is the birth of the product or service to be marketed. Once it is developed, the news that it is available must be communicated both within the organization and to potential clients. Communications aimed at developing leads then come into play, including direct mail campaigns and networking. The next stage in marketing is bringing in the new account, which requires such skills as making presentations, relationship management, and the art of persuasion. The cycle is completed when you develop the ability to keep your clients happy through service quality, which allows you to build a long-term client base in preparation for cross-selling the next new product or service. What I plan to do in the pages that follow is take you through this cycle, providing the information you need to succeed at each stage.

2

Winging It: The Result Is Crisis Management

All too often today, when people wing it and succeed, they are greeted with admiration. Their success is taken to mean that they have mixed luck and an ability to fake knowledge of some sort and come out ahead of the game. Originally, the term *winging it* was used to describe actors who relied on prompters in the wings because they hadn't learned their lines, and it was derogatory. Winging it, or bluffing, enhanced neither the performance nor the reputation of an actor performing without adequate preparation.

It is impossible to substitute winging it for planning, preparation, and practice. When people wing it, they hope everything will work out, but they do not know that it will. As a result of laziness or a tendency to operate on automatic pilot, they forget that making things work takes work. As Isaac Stern is reported to have said, "If I don't practice for one day, I can hear it. If I don't practice for two days, the orchestra can tell. And if I miss three days' practice, the public knows."

As an executive, you may have confidence in your ability to make off-the-cuff decisions; indeed, winging it may have become a habit, one you have little inclination to break because it has never created a major problem—yet. Maybe it is time you took a closer look at the dangers. Ask yourself whether you acted in the firm's best interests when, for example, you hired the new department head who is now causing so much dissension. Do you

13

remember hiring that person without having a thorough background check made because you thought the person was the best of the lot and you did not want to spend more time conducting still more interviews? If you ask yourself the right questions, you may discover that the time has come to stop winging it.

A Pervasive Problem

As an experienced manager or executive, you may be confident that in the long run your tendency to make off-the-cuff decisions has created few problems. Before you decide that it is all right to shoot from the hip so long as everything goes well most of the time, ask yourself:

- Would you trust a doctor who had a habit of prescribing medicine based on patients' descriptions of ailments rather than on examinations?
- Would you trust a financial adviser who decided which stocks to add to a portfolio on the basis of darts thrown at a stock list, even though that adviser usually came out ahead?
- Would you continue to use an attorney who came to court without the right documents time after time, even though that attorney wins more cases than he or she loses?

These are exaggerations, of course, but think of your reactions to the questions. Now ask yourself if you suffer from even a mild form of the same disease—acting without first obtaining adequate information. Also, think about the implications for your reputation if anyone could describe you as being like that doctor, adviser, or attorney.

What is most frightening is that this kind of behavior so often goes undetected until it is too late. For example, one company spent weeks drafting a proposal and preparing an oral presentation for expensive computer equipment. Getting the key customer would have meant gaining a leading position in the industry. Unfortunately, the company lost out to a competitor with far fewer qualifications. As it turned out, the losing company's presentation, after all that effort, failed because it had not addressed the prospect's major concerns—and it was presented to the wrong executive. Everyone was so concerned with getting the proposal and presentation right that no one had examined the prospect's needs in detail or had even checked carefully to find out who the key decision maker was. The elements of the effort were never viewed as a whole; the key decision makers acted too quickly, allowing instinct to take the place of investigation, analysis, and thorough planning.

Look around and then ask yourself how many times executives in your firm make important decisions with inadequate information. Look around and ask how many corporations operate without a formalized planning process or even without proper direction from senior management. How many products or services are launched without market testing or adequate information about the competition? Understanding why these types of failures are increasingly common may help you avoid them.

Doing Many Things Better

One of the problems facing today's business executives is that technological breakthroughs have accelerated the pace of change and have increased the fear of losing a competitive edge unless action is taken at full speed. As a result, executives are taking basic activities for granted and looking for quick fixes for what they perceive to be their major problems because they think there is too much to keep up with. For example, many managers have recently become obsessed with such buzzwords as "competitiveness," "quality," "productivity," and "excellence." Often, these managers have set off in new directions, developing new plans and initiating radical new programs without first determining whether all the changes were really needed. This trendy Band-Aid approach overlooks the point that changing a Band-Aid does not necessarily heal a wound. The fundamentals of business health and a cure get overlooked in the rush to change just for the sake of changing.

The whole firm can get caught up in an attempt to install a more sophisticated quality program and in the meantime let such critical basic functions as internal communications and hiring, training, and rewarding the right people slide. Buck Rodgers, a former IBM marketing executive, was quoted in a book called *Supersellers* as saying:

> The thing I stress all the time is that you have to do 1,000 things one percent better, not just one thing 1,000 percent better. It's doing the little things well, returning phone calls, saying 'thank you' to people. It sounds like a simplistic cliché, but that is the reason one organization or one person is successful and another is not. The secret is that everybody knows what they ought to be doing, but the ones who practice daily excellence are the real 'difference makers.'[1]

Attention to Fundamentals

The truth every manager must face is that if you don't control the business, the business controls you. Once that happens, things take on a life of their own—the manager becomes managed. Events take over, and the manager ends up putting out fires rather than lighting them. One executive once confessed:

> I'm really feeling like I am being managed by all the people that I interact with, that I'm losing the ability to control my own agenda, to control the events around me. There are just so many constituencies and so many different people—above me, at the same level, below me—making demands on my time, my energies. There is just no time for planning and preparation, for research, for just plain hard thinking, much less for execution.

Managers who allow this to happen are not dealing with those basic management problems that can free them from constant involvement in internal daily concerns and allow them to focus on broader problems. For example, in terms of the people who work for them, if managers hire the right people in the first place—taking the time to thoroughly interview them, check their backgrounds—and see that they are properly introduced to the firm and continually retrained, then they will have far fewer problems to distract them from the business of meeting strategic goals.

Strategic Management versus Strategic Planning

In years past, before the advent of such intense global competition, there was less need for constant control and more tolerance for error. But today it is essential for managers to pay attention to the fundamental, day-to-day activities that comprise the proper execution of a strategy. Thus, the more control executives have over details, the more time they have to focus on execution. To execute well means giving the same concern, the same focus, to each transaction that you give to the grand, overall design. That is the difference between strategic management and strategic planning. When you manage strategically, you manage everything from the overall direction of the firm to the individual execution of each operation. In fact, one of the reasons that strategic planning fell from favor some years ago was that management spent a lot of time developing strategic plans that were well thought-out but never properly executed.

A manager has to bring the same kind of professionalism, care, planning, and preparation to individual tasks as to the development of a departmental or firmwide strategy. Your ratio of successes to failures increases dramatically in proportion to the effort you put into preparing for all the many activities that make up the business day: meetings, presentations, product introductions, interviewing, hiring, and evaluating and counseling employees.

The alternative to planning and preparation is missing the business opportunity, losing the sale, damaging relationships, discouraging and losing talented people, attracting lawsuits, and wasting untold time, effort, and money. The inevitable result for your firm is a failure to reach its objectives, whether those objectives involve meeting a new business quota, positioning services or products properly in the marketplace, or achieving a competitive advantage.

Examples of failure are usually easy to spot—after the fact. If someone in your firm failed to sell a key prospect who would enable your firm to penetrate a new industry sector, you need to examine what happened and why, and then make sure it won't happen again. In other words, you must always strive for continuous improvement. Two cases of that kind of failure are worth recounting here.

First, take the case of a consultant who had an appointment with a potential client. The prospective client asked him how much it would cost to develop a software application. Because he was afraid that admitting he did not know would make him look unprepared, he decided to wing it and quoted a figure on the spot instead of going back to the office and researching the issue. Unfortunately, after returning to the office and calculating the numbers, he found that the estimate he quoted would not even cover costs. He then went back to the prospective client and told him the estimate was wrong and the price was higher. Of course, that made the prospect furious, because he had already presented the original figure to his top management. As a result, a competitor got the business, even though the competitor's estimate was about the same as the first firm's revised price.

Next, take the case of a business that hired a new head for one of its branch offices. Management was so impressed with the man's credentials and obvious poise that they put him in charge of a staff of 30 employees. In fact, they were so eager to bring him on board that they never called around and checked his reputation. In less than a year, the new man's abrasiveness decimated the staff, leaving the survivors in turmoil, and he was terminated. If the managers had bothered to check, they would have found that their new star had done similar damage in all three of his previous positions.

In both these cases, on-the-spot decisions—winging it—cost a firm dearly. That is why it makes sense to stop in your tracks every once in a while and ask, "If I had the opportunity to do it again, how could I do it better?" It is critical to treat every failure as a learning process, determining where mistakes were made not to cast blame but to understand what has to be done differently next time. If you just go ahead without a willingness to learn from your mistakes, history is bound to repeat itself.

To ensure that things improve, you must decide what changes will prevent costly mistakes. Part of that process is determining whether failures have a pattern. If you have a poor record of holding on to clients, your objective should not be to bring in more clients, thus creating a turnstile effect, but to find out why you are losing them—and then remedy your deficiencies. The objective is not to work harder, but to work smarter.

Focusing on Specific Activities

One way to change is to replace the habit of winging it with a habit of planning for each specific activity—focusing on it, researching it thoroughly, and rehearsing it (if only in your own mind). For example, when you have a meeting or an oral presentation coming up, you must do your homework. Although a particular activity may be only one small part of a grand design, it still requires the same concern and the same focus on details necessary for larger, more significant undertakings.

Walking into a meeting cold and having an unfamiliar subject sprung on you can be embarrassing and possibly devastating to your reputation. Not long ago, for example, a business executive gave a speech at a major industry symposium. Because of a lack of time, the speech was written by a professional writer, who interviewed many people for it, but who never was given a chance to discuss his findings with the executive. As a result, the executive wasn't really familiar with all the examples given. When the chairperson of the meeting suggested an impromptu question-and-answer session after the speech was given, the executive could not deal with many of the questions and ended up looking unprepared. He simply hadn't reviewed the background material and taken the time to understand more than the speech itself.

The Payoff

Winging it is a form of shooting craps. You gamble that, prepared or not, you'll be able to handle whatever turns up—sevens or snake eyes. But even inveterate gamblers recognize that the odds are stacked against them. Taking a calculated risk (for example, doing your research and making a strategic decision) is not the same as gambling. One is taking a risk after considered judgment; the other is leaving everything up to fate or the roll of the dice.

Rehearsing a presentation, following up on details, checking credentials, and the like are a small price to pay for success. Crisis management—fighting fires all of your working day—is much more expensive. Winging it leads to a loss of credibility, wastes valuable time and effort, and can damage even the most promising career.

Of course, there will always be unpleasant surprises to deal with: The world isn't perfect, and neither are all of its inhabitants. But you can reduce the number of crises that plague you (and the stress that comes with them) by maintaining discipline over those that are controllable. As stress management experts point out, you have to get control over the way you run your life and your business.

How to Start

How do you stop this runaway freight train and gain control of your day? The answer is as simple as one old Chinese proverb: A journey of 1,000 miles begins with a single step.

Since winging it has much in common with gambling, the first step is to follow the precept that Gamblers Anonymous requires of new members: Admit that you're a gambler. Once you see yourself as a gambler (rather than an astute, risk-taking business manager), you've taken that first important step. Once you've convinced yourself that you must, immediately, break out of that winging it, shoot-from-the-hip, flip-a-coin mentality, you're on the way back to executing properly.

Gamblers Anonymous tells its members that one survives by getting through the nickels and dimes of each day in order to reach the big payoff. For the manager, this means hitting long-term goals by focusing on the specifics of reaching those goals—that is, meetings, presentations, product introductions, and sales calls. It also means selecting the right people for each task, giving them the tools to do the job, motivating them, monitoring their progress, making sure communications flow both ways, and knowing what's happening each step of the way. In short, it means being prepared and executing properly.

It is not enough to know the problems caused by winging it. It is also important to know in what areas you tend to wing it most. Some fundamental questions will help you identify your particular tendencies when it comes to winging it. The questions can be divided into different categories, some involving the way you manage your time, some involving the internal operations of your firm, and some focusing on your services and your clients. Your answers to the questions in each area will tell you a lot about yourself and your management style.

Managing Yourself

- Are you in control of your time, or are you a victim of crisis management? In other words, are you managing your day, or do you let it manage you?
- How do you make decisions? Are your decisions based on meaningful information, or do you tend to make seat-of-the-pants judgments?
- Do you develop good business relationships? Do you define roles and expectations and make it clear what you expect from the beginning?

Managing Your Firm

- Are you providing a vision and direction? Do you know where the organization is going and how it is going to get there?
- How do you prepare for internal meetings? Do you make sure that each meeting has an objective and an agenda for reaching it, or do you go into meetings unprepared, assuming that you can prevent the meeting from becoming a time-wasting debating society?
- Do you prepare for applicant interviews? Have you developed an effective system for comparing and investigating job applicants, knowing in advance what qualities to look for and selecting on that basis, or are you too likely to make decisions based mainly on an applicant's appearance and personality? Some companies are in such a rush, they don't even check résumés. A survey of 200 applicants discovered that 30 percent did not give true dates of employment, while a smaller but significant group claimed college degrees they did not have.[2]

- How do you indoctrinate new employees? Do you give new employees formal descriptions of their roles and responsibilities and then provide periodic feedback on progress, or do you just throw them in the pool to see if they can swim?
- Do you provide personnel training and development? Do you make sure that the training program helps employees perform their jobs well and prepares them for advancement, or do you expect employees to learn on the job without adequate guidance?
- Do you provide performance appraisals? Do you take those appraisals seriously, offering continuous, constructive observations to help employees grow and improve, or are performance appraisals casual, once-a-year chats?
- Do you provide for management continuity? Do you plan for a succession of managers to ensure consistency and the long-term viability of each department, or do you promote mainly on the basis of seniority?

Selling Your Services and Your Clients

- Do you know your marketplace? Do you use market research to update marketing plans continually and to develop new services in response to needs of the marketplace, or are you willing to launch new services without adequate testing?
- Do you customize your proposals to a prospective client's individual needs, or do you present standard material to everyone?
- Do you produce effective sales presentations? Do you routinely probe in advance for each prospect's needs and use material that demonstrates how your service applies, or do you try to get by on dazzling graphics, a shoeshine, and a smile?

Conclusion

Just as business and sports are similar, so are executives and coaches: Executives, like coaches, enjoy talking about game plans. But in football and in business, you do not win or lose because of grand strategies, you win or lose because you take care of basics—you make a tackle or block and avoid fumbles and turnovers.

Vince Lombardi, who was one of the most successful and most quoted of coaches, stressed the fundamentals of blocking and tackling, even to veteran professionals. His precepts have proved successful season after season. Bearing this in mind, consider these questions: How many business transactions are lost because executives try to wing it without practicing the basics? How many, on the other hand, are won simply by executing the fundamentals? Before answering, ask yourself what kind of season your own firm had last year.

3

Developing and Marketing New Services: Getting off the Treadmill to Nowhere

Do you sometimes get the impression that your firm is on a treadmill—that even though everyone in it is moving faster and working harder, the organization is standing still? In today's business environment, that is not an unusual feeling. Even the strongest companies (yes, even IBM) have had trouble keeping pace with the dizzying rate of change. Many of these changes result from technological advances, such as the speed of communications, and the increasingly global economy caused by those advances.

These changes are causing businesses not only to scramble to outflank those offering similar products and services but also to find ways to adapt to and implement the marketing techniques now needed to promote their products and services. For example, not too long ago, attorneys, accountants, management consultants, bankers, advertising and public relations executives, and investment counselors, among others, counted on getting and maintaining a steady stream of business by spending time at country clubs, by attending social and civic functions, and from client referrals. But today, social contacts and referrals are not enough.

The dramatic changes that have occurred in the marketplace—thanks to mergers and acquisitions, deregulation, the proliferation of new services, the rise of major new competitors, and clients who are ever more sophisticated in their selection of new services—have forced firms to pay more and more attention to their positioning and the way in which they differentiate their offerings from those of other firms. An article in the *Wall Street Journal* emphasized the need for law firms to "understand that marketing is now as important as finance and administration" and noted that firms "are learning that marketing is difficult, complex, and delicate."[1]

At the same time, firms have to contend with the problem of the shrinking life cycle of new services. At one time, a business could launch a new service in the marketplace, anticipating that there was time to work out the bugs in its design when they were found. Today, that is unthinkable. A competitor could launch a perfect version of the service tomorrow and capture an important market share; by the time you have an acceptable service, it may be obsolete. Moreover, innovative companies find it increasingly difficult to maintain a hard-earned market share. Given competitive intelligence, a rapid response capability, and technological advances, other companies are able to clone a service rapidly and get it to the marketplace with little risk and at little or no cost in research and development. Thus, just as you succeed in introducing an idea, the other company is there, offering the same thing at a lower cost. After all, that company does not have to factor money spent on research and development into their cost structure.

Recognizing the Problem and Finding the Solution

The first part of the problem is getting your organization to face the fact that even if the status quo is currently profitable, it may not be in the future. You must convince everyone that sooner or later your organization will find itself on a treadmill to nowhere, struggling just to keep up.

There is no single answer to the questions raised by the changes and developments in the marketplace. But one thing is obvious:

It is critical to develop new services continually and to market them effectively with strong marketing strategies, clearly defined niches, and careful positioning. At the same time, it is essential to be innovative and flexible—always ready to adapt to changes in the marketplace. The motto "If it ain't broke, don't fix it" is a sure path to mediocrity in today's economic marketplace.

There is no formula for innovation. So many factors are involved that it is hardly surprising that most innovations never succeed. In 1978 the Denver Research Institute, under the auspices of the National Science Foundation, examined 200 innovations that failed. The study indicated that "failures of management and marketing together accounted for half of the 200 innovations in the sample that faltered or failed. . . . Not surprising, perhaps, but disturbing—over one-third of the management errors involved market factors that management could have controlled."[2]

But even though there is no guaranteed recipe for success, it is useful to pay close attention to the marketing and management issues that apply to new product and service development. Experience shows that four general areas are vital to developing a new service, launching it successfully, and defending its position:

- selecting the service or product
- leadership, management style, and group dynamics
- strategy
- execution

Selecting the Service or Product

There are three traditional approaches for entering a market. In the product-driven approach, a company starts with a service or product it has already developed and tries to find a market for it. In a resource-driven approach, a company takes its inherent strengths in human and other resources and then finds the best way to employ them. In the market-driven approach, a company identifies opportunities through research and then develops a service that fills perceived customer needs.

Both the product- and resource-driven methods have serious flaws. Clients may not need or want the products or services no matter how excellent they are, and no amount of effort will make people demand what they know they do not want. Moreover, services once in demand may no longer have any relevance and may no longer bring in business. Much of this means recognizing that significant past investments in strategic resources (for example, having opened a new office when the market was booming or having trained personnel in soon-to-be-outdated technologies) may have to be written off as irrelevant in today's market. Sticking with them can be even more costly.

These are the major problems that arise with product- or resource-driven approaches. Psychologist Abraham Maslow described them succinctly: "People who are only good with hammers see every problem as a nail." Other common pitfalls that develop when using these approaches are:

- Reacting too precisely to the demands of today's market, thus rendering the service obsolete before it reaches the general market.
- Being so immersed in the technology of developing the product that there is little potential for profit (and in addition, in the case of the service, insignificant application for the client).
- Creating a service in a vacuum (without market testing) or on the basis of outdated experience.
- Focusing too heavily on the competition and attempting to match service for service or product for product. The result is likely to be the development of a me-too service in an already overcrowded market.

The market-driven approach clearly offers advantages over the product- and resource-driven approaches because it is the only one based on the actual needs of prospective clients. But how can you find out what services are needed? First, set the stage, and then keep your eyes and your mind open. Attitude is important. Actively and sincerely solicit and encourage everyone you talk to, to think about and report new ideas. Roger von Oech, author and creative consultant, has compared looking for new ideas to prospecting for gold. He warns that "if you look in the same old places, you'll find tapped out veins."[3]

New ideas are everywhere. But if you are to hear them, you have to create the proper atmosphere—one in which you are perceived as receptive to suggestions from anyone at any level in your organization and from people outside the organization. You must also set up a mechanism to gather feedback from suppliers, your clients, or your clients' customers on what you are offering and on what they need. Also give some thought to how existing services can be modified, improved, or line extended and how they can be applied to new markets. Analyze also whether current services can be applied to new markets. Finally, keep up steady, formal or informal market research among those you have not yet reached, searching always for promising new ideas in the responses you get.

All too often, management will fail to act on even the very best new ideas out of the all-too-human tendency to resist change. The most common rationalizations for not trying something new are:

- We've always done it this way.
- It's too radical.
- That's contrary to policy.
- Can you guarantee that it will work?
- It won't work in our industry.
- We don't have the time.
- The last idea you came up with wasn't so great, why should I listen to you this time?
- If it's such a great idea, why didn't anyone come up with it before?

If these excuses sound at all familiar, you must find the courage to brush them aside and plunge into the unknown on occasion.

Refusing to try something new can prove costly—and embarrassing. Before giving in to the temptation to play it safe, ask yourself if you want to be remembered as the person who turned down the idea of the century. Do you want to be remembered along with the Western Union executive who turned down the patent for the telephone or the executive who told Steve Wozniak that Hewlett-Packard wasn't interested in personal computers only to see him go off and found Apple Computer?

Of course, not every idea is a good one. Choosing among possibilities is a balancing act between being too cautious—which can, for example, lead to entering the market late, being a me-too player, and having to discount fees—and grasping every fad that comes along, spreading resources too thin. The following questions can help you to evaluate the potential of a new service:

- Does it leverage the existing skills, resources, experience, and image of the organization?
- Is it transferable—that is, is it broadly based rather than dependent on the expertise of any single individual?
- Does it offer longevity?
- Can it be differentiated from other services already in the marketplace?
- Does it fit in properly with the future of the organization— that is, will it be possible to develop without making major structural changes?

Leadership, Management Style, and Group Dynamics

Good management is a critical ingredient in the mix that creates a successful new service. It is a complex blend of leadership, management style, and group dynamics, each of which plays a specific role. A major leadership role is filled by the service champion—the single individual who spearheads the project. Then, when the development of the service calls for more team action, management style and group dynamics come into the picture. In addition, and of equal importance, is the role senior management plays.

The Right Kind of Leadership at Every Level

Keep in mind that at different phases of a new product, different types of leaders are necessary. A person who can start a business from scratch, for example, often does not have the skills to manage it once it is operating. One of the many examples of this is Convergent Technologies. Once one of Silicon Valley's most successful companies, its growth was so rapid that management lost control. Allen Michaels, president of the company, has candidly admitted, "I learned—painfully—that I'll never be a successful manager. Some people are good at operating big companies; I'm good at starting companies, creating life where there was none."[4] In a variant on that idea, it is clear that those who manage a company and oversee new service development and those who develop a service play very different roles.

Senior Management. In developing new services, senior management's most important role is probably a supportive one. It provides direction, sets guidelines, and establishes clear and consistent expectations. It also must lend emotional support and provide encouragement to the development team. However, while it should monitor progress and establish appropriate reward systems, senior management should not be involved in day-to-day operations. Particularly confusing and harmful is the hands-on/hands-off style of some executives who delegate a task, then take over two weeks later, only to leave again.

Management can do much to create an environment that nourishes new ideas by emphasizing the value of personal growth, risk taking, and continuing education. For example, when group members are weak in an area, such as strategy development, public speaking, marketing, or interpersonal skills, management should encourage them to acquire that skill through formal or informal training and should make arrangements for that training. At the same time, management should encourage the entire organization to support the development group and stand by to provide assistance when it is needed.

Management should make a firm and realistic commitment to a new service before starting any development on it. It is a mistake to abandon a project prematurely. Realistically, since an innovation cannot be expected to generate immediate profits, it is a mistake to judge its success too soon or to expect it to match returns with well-established services too early. Moreover, a new service is an investment that usually requires heavy up-front costs, for market research, personnel training, marketing promotion, and the short-term revenue loss of people reassigned to perform these jobs.

Sometimes even a company's best efforts to market a product fail. Then the decision must be made on whether to pull the product or try something else. Sometimes modifications in a product and the way it is marketed can make all the difference. Procter & Gamble made such a switch midstream on its Pringles potato chips, which many thought of as the Edsel of the Procter & Gamble product line. Management decided that, with so much invested already, it made sense to go ahead with a last-ditch salvage operation before abandoning the product. The recipe was changed, new varieties added, and the packaging modified to try to attract a larger market share.[5]

On the other hand, some companies, such as 3M, that adhere to a philosophy of conducting numerous small experiments do not run the risk of an all-or-nothing research endeavor. They do not become set in their ways or assume that once an avenue is pursued there is no turning back, which can occur when, for example, projects are overfunded. They would rather conduct a small trial than spend months writing a proposal. They do not set up bureaucracies, they remain extremely flexible, and they maintain a belief in continuous improvement.

Shortcuts are also wasteful. For example, in order to succeed, a new service must be properly prepared and given adequate support. Management must ensure that market research is carried out. Without test marketing, chances are that the service developed does not deal with the most important needs of the client. Other common mistakes management makes are abandoning a project when it meets its first hurdle (it may be inches from turning into a real winner), developing a service in response to a fad where the firm's commitment may be too weak to produce a viable service, developing a service that does not fit the firm's image of the business it is in, or failing to protect the team from the organization's bureaucratic policies and internal barriers.

Tom Peters warns us to "take heed of the words of Fred Brooks, legendary chief designer of IBM's pathbreaking System 360: 'How does a project get to be a year behind schedule? One day at a time.' The accumulation of little items, each too 'trivial' to trouble the boss with, is a prime cause of miss-the-market delays.

As boss, you must consciously view yourself as basher-in-chief of small barriers and facilitator-in-chief of trivial aids to action rather than 'the great planner.' "[6]

The Initiator. The second level of critical leadership in service development is that of the service champion, the individual who spearheads the project. The best initiators are self-appointed, not designated; they naturally have a vested interest in making the service a success. These individuals tend to have a definable set of personal qualities:

- *Vision.* A clear perception of goals and readily visible belief in what is being done; "all organizations depend on the existence of shared meanings and interpretations of reality, which facilitate coordinated action."[7]
- *Passion.* An inner drive to forge ahead at all costs; a must-succeed attitude.
- *Independence.* A sense of self that allows these individuals to work alone or create synergy while working with others.
- *High Energy Level.* Staying power and the ability to maintain drive at all times, which inspires others to do the same.
- *High Achiever.* The determination to be the best, to overcome all obstacles and find a way to succeed.
- *Self-discipline.* These individuals do not need to be prodded; they set their own goals and schedules and meet them.
- *Self-confidence.* These people are willing to take chances and go against conventional wisdom.
- *Delegate Authority.* Such individuals ferret out the strengths of others and assign appropriate tasks to them, bringing out their best.
- *Listening Skills.* They do not force ideas on others, stifling their creativity.
- *Interpersonal Skills.* The ability to motivate and communicate with others, forging strong teams.
- *Credibility.* They have the required background, experience, and know-how to do the job and ensure the respect of those who work with them.

• *Trust.* They can instill an atmosphere of teamwork, caring, and respect for one another.

Management Style and Group Dynamics

Another aspect of good management is the handling of group dynamics, which is affected by general management style. When a group develops a service, its management style should be to encourage every member to participate. Team spirit should prevail—an emphasis on "we" instead of on "I." Although individual efforts deserve support, the team has to be motivated by a common vision and must work to achieve a common goal. Group members must know from ongoing actions that they will be praised for their individual accomplishments and rewarded for their collective successes. This means, for example, that senior management should from the beginning use devices such as congratulatory memos or pats on the back or something akin to the legendary Friday "get-togethers" at Tandem Computer to build teamwork.

It is important that success be evaluated in terms of specific goals and objectives and not on arbitrary, subjective standards. The evaluation process should be ongoing, with continual monitoring, rather than a once-a-year event. Individuals can be evaluated more effectively, and the decision-making process can be enhanced, by breaking down the bureaucracy so that members of the development team are responsible for decisions in their designated areas. In this way, those closest to a situation have decision-making authority; even though they are encouraged to solicit advice from colleagues, they are not subject to stultifying consensus management.

Another way to strengthen the group and enhance the decision-making process is to be careful to choose people with diverse backgrounds. This encourages a variety of viewpoints, a sure way to generate positive energy. Of course, it also requires considerable freedom of expression and an experimental environment. Rather than trying for the home run, it is often more expedient to make a lot of base hits, thus moving ahead by testing your assumptions in small stages.

When it comes to group dynamics, the most important element

is open and continual communication, which is enhanced by placing the team in close physical proximity. People should not be afraid to take stands. They should be given enough support, with the firm's blessing, so that they know that failure is an opportunity to learn and that continuous improvement, even through failure, can be a key to success. The group should remain flexible, allowing roles to evolve and members to wear different hats as the need arises. This will allow members to become leaders as the service cycle develops. Indeed, it is critical that the group remain flexible enough to shift emphasis from area to area—for example, from product development to marketing, from quality control to service delivery.

Strategy

The aim of strategy is not fighting. Strategy is about creating positions that are inherently superior so that when you fight the odds are strongly in your favor. Developing a strategy for marketing your service should not be left entirely in the hands of professional strategists. Everyone responsible for delivering and supporting the service or product should be personally committed to the success of the venture and should be willing and encouraged to participate fully in the planning process.

Developing Effective Strategic Plans

Finding a way to strike a balance between sufficient planning and too much planning is difficult. As Roger von Oech has written, "If you spend too much time warming up, you'll miss the race. If you don't warm up at all, you may not finish the race."[8]

Many service development groups spend so much time gathering information about markets, statistical trends, and data on their competition that their plans become enormously thick, unmanageable documents. According to Jack Welch, chief executive officer of General Electric, what is needed is an "all-out war" against "the cramping artifacts that pile up in the dusty attics of century-old companies: reports, meetings, rituals, approvals, and forests of paper that seem necessary until they are removed."[9]

Those creating plans seem to forget that risk can never be eliminated by excessive planning. All too often those huge planning documents end up sitting on shelves and collecting dust until the following year, when they need to be updated. In between, nothing is done.

Remember that strategic planning should not only set goals but should include tactics to accomplish them. A plan is only valuable when it is action-oriented and when its progress can be continually monitored and updated. A plan should not be measured by its newness, bulk, or complexity. It also should not cause planners to ignore a proven approach that would work as well or better. The cry of "Let's try something different" sometimes can be a mistake, causing the obvious to be overlooked in favor of the obscure. One can learn from the past, from one's own experiences, and from those of other companies. There is no need to reinvent the wheel.

How to Evaluate Your Strategic Plan

Beware of vague objectives and hollow plans. It sounds impressive to say you are going to "be the best," to "increase business significantly," to "target *Fortune 500* executives," or to "dominate the market." But do you know how you will accomplish those objectives? What specific actions are required, and how will progress be measured? Many plans create goals without strategies or establish quantifiable objectives without monitoring systems. In the worst cases of all, a service is developed in its entirety, but an organization's infrastructure is not changed in response nor are personnel trained to support the new service. Remember that a plan is only as good as an organization's ability to execute it, which is reflected in results.

Once a plan has been developed, it needs to be evaluated in terms of the organization's ability to carry it out. In "A Critical Analysis of the Vietnam War," Colonel Harry G. Summers, Jr., described the principles of military strategy. This examination can be adapted to strategic business management as well. When so applied it provides the basis for a series of questions that explore:

- *Objective*—that is, the purpose of the enterprise. Once you know the purpose, you can ask, "Is the objective clearly defined, and is it based on a realistic view of the marketplace?"
- *Initiative*—that is, the organization's ability to set the pace in the field. Does your plan allow you to jump ahead of your competitors; for example, will your strategy help you grab the competitive initiative?
- *Mass*—that is, how well the plan allows you to concentrate the company's resources at critical points. Are you spreading your resources too thin?
- *Economy*—that is, how skillfully and prudently resources are used. How well does the plan allocate resources to the main tasks? Does it allocate enough to allow an edge over the competition? Are you trying to be all things to all people?
- *Flexibility*—that is, the plan's ability to allow you to shift resources easily when they are needed at different stages. Can the firm react quickly to rapidly changing circumstances? Can the firm's compensation plan handle changes that will occur?
- *Unity of leadership*—that is, promotion of coordinated efforts by all participants toward a common goal. If you ask 15 people in what direction the firm is heading, does each give the same response?
- *Security*—that is, the ability to keep the competition from knowing what you are doing. Is it clear to everyone what information has to be kept secure?
- *Surprise*—that is, does the organization have the ability to strike the competition at a time and place for which it is unprepared? Do you have enough speed, deception, and competitive intelligence to prevent your competitors from cloning your services?
- *Simplicity*—that is, the ability to be clearly understood. Is the plan as simple as it can be? Have you reduced the potential for misunderstanding?

- *Speed*—that is, can you mobilize forces and react at will? Do bureaucracy, consensus management, undefined responsibility, and political infighting reduce your capacity to move quickly?
- *Communication*—that is, has the plan been made available to those who need to know? Does it make clear what they need to know to carry out their responsibilities? Is communication upward as well as downward?
- *Commitment*—that is, do employees feel that they are part of the venture, willing to march forward? Or is a small group dictating action?

Before carrying out your strategic plan, a checklist including questions like these should be set up and distributed to those involved in the strategy for developing the service. Each individual should sit down with the list and give an opinion of how well each part has been dealt with in the plan. Comparing answers will reveal a great deal and allow the plan to be changed before it is too late.

Developing a Plan to Win the Marketing War

To get results in a competitive market, it is necessary to focus on differentiating and positioning the service. As Theodore Levitt of the Harvard Business School once said, "Being 'all things to all people' is a recipe for strategic mediocrity and below-average performance, because it means that a firm has no competitive advantage at all."

To achieve competitive advantage, you have to set priorities and make choices. General Electric's Jack Welch said in an article in *Fortune* that "the job of a leader is to take the available resources—human and financial—and allocate them rigorously. Not to spread them out evenly, like butter on bread. That's what bureaucrats do. It takes courage and tough-mindedness to pick the bets, put resources behind them, articulate the vision to the employees, and explain why you said yes to this one and no to that one."[10] Keep the following questions in mind when you find yourself scrambling to get the service out the door:

- Who is the client and what does he or she need?
- What makes the service unique?
- Why is the service better than what your competitors offer?
- How can your firm defend its position in the marketplace?

The executive contemplating the best strategy for winning a major battle is like the general thinking about tactics. Carl von Clausewitz, perhaps the most perceptive writer on war ever, wrote in *On War,* "The first, the supreme, the most far-reaching act of judgment that the statesman and commander have to make is to establish . . . the kind of war on which they are embarking." The same is true of the executive. It is critical for executives to decide which fronts to attack on and how to position their businesses in that part of the market where they have a competitive advantage strong enough to discourage other firms from attacking. In particular, the tactic of *mass* can be borrowed from military strategy. Former Assistant Secretary of the Army William E. Peacock defined this concept as "the concentration of superior [resources] . . . at the point of decision in a struggle between two or more corporate giants."[11]

One might choose, for example, to concentrate resources on two or three services instead of many, to target specific industries in which to develop a real expertise or niche, or to select key geographical locations where you can marshal superior manpower. By massing resources, even a small firm can achieve a superior market position, because it is easier to find success with a spotlight than with a floodlight.

When entering markets, executives can also call on military tactics by picking the right offensive strategies. These include frontal assaults, flanking attacks, encirclement, bypass attacks, and guerrilla warfare. Each of these forms of attack can be applied in business.

In brief, the frontal assault militarily is a head-on attack in which an aggressor attacks its opponent in force. In business it occurs when a firm matches another firm service for service, price for price, promotion for promotion, ad for ad, and so forth. If such a strategy is to succeed, the attacker must be able to overpower the defender.

In the military, a flanking attack involves forcing the enemy to try to meet what looks like a frontal attack while really moving in on troops guarding the rear and sides of the main military force—the positions where it is weakest. In business, the flanking attack is usually carving out a geographic or segmental niche—that is, picking locations in which an opponent is weak to launch a service or find services to provide that your competitors do not provide.

A military encirclement is a large-scale simultaneous offensive against an enemy on a number of fronts. It makes sense when the attacking army is stronger and believes it can finish off the enemy. In business, encirclement involves meeting any service the competitor comes up with, with a similar service and getting into as many markets as possible.

A bypass attack is somewhat different. It involves avoiding any major encounters, thus allowing the offensive group to build its strength or, by solidifying its position in small fringe areas, to place itself in the strongest possible position for later encounters. In business, it involves getting into easier markets (such as un-related services) until you have built a sufficient base, or getting into markets in geographical areas where a competitor is weak.

The final offensive tactic is guerrilla warfare. In the military as well as in the business world, such an attack is launched by a weaker, smaller group on a larger one. In the military, it involves such tactics as small attacks on supplies and on small ill-protected outposts. In business, it involves tactics such as stealing executives or cutting prices for a short time to arouse interest.[12]

Military tactics can be adapted in business in many ways. Several specific strategies can be used to enter a new market successfully:

- Concentrate on getting one major account first. Then use that successful base as a stepping-stone to obtain new business.
- Concentrate on services that differentiate your firm significantly, emphasizing its existing image and the inherent characteristics of the service.
- Cross-sell new services to existing clients.
- Develop synergy among your services to secure the natural follow-on sales. For example, in consulting, a strategic plan-

ning service would coordinate well with a systems implementation service.

- Develop geographical pockets of clients, and use personal references and local reputation to broaden your base from there.

- Enter a market by first producing ancillary products (supplies) before the big push into the primary market (hardware).

Execution

A plan is only as good as an organization's ability to execute it. Successful execution requires paying attention to detail and not ignoring the obvious. In short, all of the required resources must be aligned with the goal of launching a new service. The refrain "We've always done it this way" can be a barrier. To succeed, you may have to reevaluate your organization's structure, provide more effective incentives, review manpower requirements, revise channels of distribution, enhance educational programs, increase selling skills, or experiment with new marketing techniques. The entire organization must be evaluated, compensated, and rewarded for achieving the marketing goals for the new service or product. A reward system that works at cross-purposes with your objectives will hinder the success of an enterprise; so can failing to let people know that it exists.

Marketing communications, such as brochures, advertising, direct mail, seminars, and speeches, are a necessary aspect of any effort to launch a new service, as will be seen in Chapter 4. Too many marketing communication efforts are flawed because they are haphazard, rushed, or based on imprecise thinking. Communication has to be targeted and focused. Strategy, message, and vehicle have to work together to achieve specific objectives. Marketing communications is a means to an end, not an end in itself. This applies to communicating internally to your personnel and externally to both your existing clients and to new prospects.

Before launching a new service, make sure that all the operations in the firm are able to adapt to the sudden diversion of resources and attention. There should be no inconsistencies between resources and objectives. For example, it is self-defeating to attempt to gain a presence in all major markets when only two offices are capable of delivering a service. If a law firm has a majority of first-year people, it is not likely to have the credibility to target *Fortune 500* clients for a new service. Without the proper training, it is unwise to expect inexperienced staff to manage large, complex engagements.

You also need to balance your marketing efforts between the long-range and short-range. How much time should you spend on bringing in new business today, as opposed to developing services for tomorrow? Even when business is good, it is dangerous to rest on your laurels. Although it is tempting to ignore future business when you are busy with today's clients, unless you take steps to develop new clients, you may be in for an unpleasant surprise when the current work ends or if you lose a client. For example, if you do not work to ensure a constant flow of business, your firm will frequently experience peaks and valleys, creating tremendous anxiety and even causing intolerable employee turnover.

You can avoid these potential pitfalls and keep on track when launching a new service in the marketplace in a number of ways. To start, ask yourself the following questions:

- Are members of your firm who serve existing clients knowledgeable about the new service, its applications, and its benefits? (If not, they will not be able to convey the appropriate message to their audience.)
- Do members of your firm have confidence in your group's ability to deliver the service? (If not, they will not recommend it to their clients.)
- Is your firm so concerned with its day-to-day operations that it will not take the time to develop a long-lasting service?
- Are some people so unaccustomed to prospecting that they fail to follow up leads or, when working on long-term business prospects, become frustrated and give up?
- Do some members of your firm feel so uncomfortable making cold calls and prospecting that they spend most of their time

preparing marketing materials that are ineffective and never make direct contact with prospects?

- Is your marketing communications material so generic that it does not address real client needs?
- Might faulty market research result in targeting the wrong audience—people who do not need the service or people who are not involved in decision making?
- Will clients' initial interest in the service wane because, after exploring it at greater length, they find it lacking?
- Are your available resources so minimal that they fail to make an impact on the market?

As the service cycle evolves and the product or service reaches the market, your employees must monitor progress in a systematic way. Unless you monitor on a continual basis, you invite the danger of not knowing that changes are needed until it is too late to do anything. A day-to-day approach keeps the group on track.

A Checklist: Ten Musts for Developing New Services

The magnitude of the stakes when introducing new services can be illustrated by the following anecdote:

A frog can be boiled to death by slowly bringing the water to a boil, thus keeping the rate of increase in water temperature just below the frog's threshold of noticeable difference. In effect, while the environment catastrophically changes around the frog, it sits there dumb and happy until it is too late to jump out of the pot.[13]

To avoid the fate of the frog, a firm and its management must:

1. Know the market, the competition, its needs, and its capabilities and limitations.
2. Encourage new ideas, and objectively decide which ones are worth pursuing.
3. Set realistic objectives for new services, establish priorities, and act on them.

4. Commit the resources that are needed to achieve its objectives.

5. Encourage a leader with the ability and the authority to get a job done.

6. Take time to plan, and then plan to act.

7. Differentiate its service, based on the needs of the marketplace, its strengths, and its competitors' weaknesses.

8. Develop the proper communication vehicles to promote the service both internally and in the marketplace.

9. Foster the climate, and build the organizational structures and incentives to provide the optimal chance for success.

10. Evaluate continually, learn from the successes or failures of its efforts, and modify its actions accordingly.

4

Marketing Communications: A Means to an End

"Our proposal is a real winner; it's 78 pages long." "This advertisement is fantastic; it's winning all kinds of awards." "The seminar was a great success—85 people attended it." These statements, all too common in many organizations, are an indication of unfocused initial objectives.

A proposal is not necessarily clear and does not necessarily address a client's real needs just because it is long. An advertising award given for beauty of design or clever copy has nothing to do with an advertisement's effectiveness in increasing business or enhancing image. Good attendance at a seminar indicates only that the campaign to get people to attend was successful, not that the seminar, which was meant to attract new business, was successful.

In order to evaluate the success of a given marketing tool, you have to measure the results you get against the objective of the form of communication used. For example, when you measure its effectiveness, you must keep in mind whether the marketing vehicle you chose was meant to sell your firm's services or products or whether it was meant to develop an image.

Too many marketing communication efforts (advertising, brochures, seminars, newsletters, direct mail, speeches) are developed in a haphazard or even arbitrary way. They are rushed, poorly planned, or based on imprecise thinking. For a marketing communications tool to be effective, the strategy, the message, and the vehicle used must all work together to achieve specific goals and objectives. Marketing communications is a means to an end, not an end in itself.

Ten All-Too-Common Mistakes

Instead of keeping an eye on the purpose of a promotion, eager marketers often run headlong in the wrong direction, focusing on peripheral issues and missing their targets. The analogy of archery comes to mind. If you don't keep your eye on the target, all the physical strength in the world and the best bow and arrow will not help you get a bull's-eye.

Mistakes are all too easy to make. The following are typical wrong approaches to a marketing campaign.

- "Their program really worked. Let's model our next campaign after theirs." A campaign that worked for someone else might not work when applied to a different project. Take a fresh look at each situation and determine the best way to achieve your objectives.
- "Let's get something out there quickly and then, after the business comes in, develop a strategy and do it the right way." This is known as the ready-fire-aim approach. It is foolish to evaluate a program more on its speedy production than on its effectiveness. Timing is important, but there has to be a balance between mapping out an effective strategy and executing it on time.
- "Before looking at the campaign, let's look at the cost." Although cost is important, marketing campaigns should not be chosen solely on that basis. Cost is only one consideration. Other factors, such as a campaign's purpose, audience, and strategy, are just as critical.
- "Let's produce an elaborate brochure that will knock them dead." Elaborate vehicles are often chosen for the wrong

reasons—to impress business associates or to emulate the competition. If something expensive isn't truly needed, why take the risk of overwhelming the audience?

- "The more material potential clients get, the better the chance of winning new business." Weight is never more important than substance. Indeed, in most cases, a lean message that is to the point is superior to a longer, more tedious one.

- "Use up the budget this year, so at least that much will be allocated for next year." If it looks as if there will be a budget surplus at the year's end, don't just spend money so that the campaign won't look overbudgeted or to prevent a smaller allocation the following year. Request what you think you need. A surplus can show that you are careful with the firm's resources.

- "Now is as good a time as any to advertise." Don't let the marketing approach become more important than communication goals. For example, national advertising isn't a good idea when your product is available only in limited geographic areas, not throughout the country. Such widespread advertising could actually harm business as a whole. People who become irritated by a firm's inability to deliver one service might reject other services it offers.

- "We're not certain who the audience is, so why not send it to everybody?" Besides the obvious waste involved, this can cause the communications to fail. The material will be too general, will not be aimed at the specific needs the service can actually meet (which should be known through the market research effort conducted before the service was developed). Instead of spending, say, $30,000 to reach everyone, it is much more effective to define an audience, spend $10,000 to reach it, and spend the remaining $20,000 reinforcing the message.

- "The service will surely sell because it is technically superior to anything on the market." This is a case of emphasizing product features rather than benefits. Give customers what *they* need, not what you want them to have. Products don't sell because they're technically superior; they sell because they fulfill a client's need.

- "Managers will develop the materials; secretaries will handle the details." Nitty-gritty details may not be as interesting as the creative aspects of a project; however, execution is as important as a concept. Programs do not succeed without follow-up. A good plan that is well implemented will virtually always beat a great plan that is poorly implemented.

Take heart—most of these mistakes are all too common. They are the result of well-intentioned but half-baked attempts to communicate that usually end in wasted time and money if not in downright failure. The basic problem underlying all of them is a lack of attention to the basic issues in marketing communications. In one way or another, each represents a way in which you can get caught up in irrelevant details or blind alleys, in means rather than ends. The efforts are hit-or-miss instead of purposeful and well planned.

As in many areas of business, it is important to take a strong position and establish priorities in order to create a successful marketing communications program. Instead of moving firmly in one direction, many people like to spread their risks and go in many directions at the same time. Such a lack of economy of focus dilutes the power of any campaign, a danger in business (as noted in Chapter 3), as well as in the military. As Harvard professor Thomas Bonoma notes in *The Marketing Edge,* "An inability to make tough and inequitable choices among marketing subfunctions often produces the very mediocrity management hopes to avoid."[1]

Planning a Successful Marketing Communications Program

There are no shortcuts in planning a successful marketing communications campaign. The firm's marketing division must carefully review possible alternatives. Then it must make decisions in five specific areas: purpose, audience, strategy, message, and execution.

Purpose

Having a clear purpose for a marketing campaign may sound obvious, yet lack of attention to purpose is the most common and the most deadly error of all. Besides guiding you in the right direction, the purpose is also a benchmark against which the quality of work and the magnitude of achievement can be measured. To define the purpose, ask a key question: What are you trying to achieve?

This question cannot be avoided. Answering it requires taking a stand and setting priorities. Moreover, since the goals of a marketing program are an outgrowth of the goals of the business itself, a marketing campaign raises critical questions within an organization and may even be a means of forcing senior management to issue clear statements of goals. Once known, goals allow communication managers to take the first step in defining a firm's communications needs. Clear goals also allow members of the communications team to work together toward a common end instead of attempting to achieve their own independent aims. For example, a communications goal could be introducing a new product or service, providing information, creating demand, developing a prospect base, reaching pinpointed markets, building client relations, or promoting a special event. Choosing a purpose and defining it are the foundation of a successful communications effort.

Audience

Like gift giving, communication involves two parties—the communicator, who gives, and the audience, which receives. A giver can focus on what he or she would like to have or on what the recipient would really like to receive. Obviously, someone who focuses on what the recipient wants is more likely to buy a gift that will be treasured and appreciated. Similarly, success in marketing communications depends largely on the communicator's sensitivity to the audience. To focus on the audience—that is, the market for the service being offered—you must ask such questions as: Is the market broad-based, or should you try to capture a small niche? Is the market global, national, regional, or local? Do large, medium, or small companies make the best prospects? Is there a particular functional area or organizational level within those companies that makes decisions about products or services? Who influences decisions no matter what the level? Is your firm currently communicating with this group? Ask yourself two important things when thinking about your audience: Are you thinking the way the recipient of your services thinks, and is your material aimed directly at the recipient?

Step into Another's Shoes.   The more you concentrate on your audience, rather than on your services or ideas, the more successful communication will be. One good example of how to go wrong is provided by a lecturer whose audience becomes bored and restless because they are not interested in the subject matter or cannot relate it to their own personal interests. It does not matter how good the content of a speech is if an audience isn't interested. An audience can also be turned off by too much information. Numerous details or endless statistics can numb an audience, causing them to stop paying attention. Marketing communications can make the same mistakes.

To make sure you are communicating effectively, do everything possible to find out how your audience thinks. Some formal or informal market research will probably be needed. Learn about the key issues the audience faces. This might involve attending industry trade shows and conventions, participating in trade associations, and reading annual reports and executive speeches. It might also call for evaluating how competitors have positioned themselves in advertisements and brochures and analyzing why they succeeded or failed in their efforts.

Keep in mind that the same message will not appeal to everyone. In fact, people will interpret information differently depending on several factors: the impact it has on their own business unit or department within the firm; their level in the organization, and thus their perspectives; how relevant the information is to them personally and to their careers; and the vantage point from which they look at it—that is, their backgrounds and previous personal experiences.

Those in the sales department, for example, will have different interests and considerations from those in the controller's office. A top executive will be interested in the overall picture, while a middle manager might focus on technical details. Someone who is trained in quantitative methods will want to see numerical analysis, whereas an individual who is interested in concepts might prefer a verbal explanation.

Narrow the Field. In general, the more focused the campaign, the more successful it will be. Focus is a result of concentrating on narrow targets and practicing segmentation.

The rewards for narrowing the field and concentrating on a clearly defined audience are many. The financial return will be greater, since money is being spent to communicate with people who have a higher probability of purchasing a service. Messages can be customized so that they specifically address a prospect's real needs. This will allow the development of a highly focused and coordinated campaign in which advertising, direct mail, sales presentations, and other vehicles can complement one another and help your firm carve out a position in the marketplace. Finally, the more targeted the campaign, the more easily and successfully you can reinforce the message and follow up on leads.

One way of narrowing the field is by industry. Material that is specific to a particular industry and that draws on real-life examples is much more meaningful to clients than generic material that tries to appeal to the masses. Industry-specific communications will also reflect an understanding of the needs and concerns of an audience and demonstrate a commitment to the industry.

Segmentation in markets can be based on such demographic variables as geographic locations, income, sex, age, education, religion, and product usage. Industrial markets can be segmented by such criteria as geographic location, size, type of business, and use of a specific product or service.

Strategy

Once the goal of the campaign is defined and the audience identified, plans can be made to accomplish specific goals.

Positioning in the Marketplace.   The first step in developing a communications strategy is to perform an audit of the communications materials that the audience is currently seeing. You need to know what messages your audience is reading or hearing and who is sending them. In their best-selling book *Positioning: The Battle for Your Mind,* Al Ries and Jack Trout noted that today's audiences are like "supersaturated sponges," overloaded with information and resistant to absorbing any more:

> With only 6 percent of the world's population, America consumes 57 percent of the world's advertising. . . . Each year some 30,000 books are published in America . . . which doesn't sound like a lot until you realize it would take 17 years of reading 24 hours a day just to finish one year's output. . . . The TV picture is really a still picture that changes 30 times a second, which means that the average family is exposed to some 795,000 television pictures a day.[2]

Amidst all this clutter, you must find a way to get an audience's attention. The tactics you choose will depend, at least in part, on the number and the nature of the competition: Are there many or few? Are there clear market leaders, or are all the contenders considered equal? Notice who your major competitors are and how they differentiate themselves.

When you conduct your audit, you must be sure to include your firm and its communications in it, being as objective as possible when assessing how the audience perceives your firm and its products. You can learn from your own past successes and failures, as well as from the successes or failures of other firms that have tried to achieve similar objectives. What should be kept the same? What should be changed? How can you improve on past experience?

As David Ogilvy noted, "The results of your campaign depend less on how we write your advertising than on how the product is positioned."[3] That is why it is critical to devise the proper strategy to differentiate yourself from the crowd. Although it is useful to study your competitors, it is possible to become too focused on them. A preoccupation with competitors means that you are much more likely to be a follower than a leader. It is important to be honest with yourself about whether your message is unique or whether it will be confused with another message.

Elements of the Plan. The following is a checklist of additional points to consider in completing a communications strategy.

- *Timing.* Is time a factor? When does the client make decisions? Is the business cyclical? Might your company have to respond to a shift in a competitor's strategy, pricing, or new service announcement? Are your own future service announcements a factor?

- *Geography.* Should your message be communicated nationally with a big splash or rolled out area by area over a period of time? A national campaign would be counterproductive if you are test marketing a service or if you cannot deliver it nationwide. As explained in Chapter 3, there are many benefits in massing your resources to attack a specific target.

- *Method.* Is it more effective to communicate with an audience in writing, in person, or by telephone? This depends, in part, on the size of the audience. You may not be able to see everyone personally in an audience of 3,000 people. The enormous cost differences of different methods also have to be taken into account.

- *Vehicle.* Often at some point in the planning process the right vehicle will suggest itself. When it does, be careful not to dismiss it because it has never been tried. If you always stick to previous successes and are afraid to try something new, you can miss wonderful new opportunities. Consider each situation from a fresh perspective, and match the vehicle to the need. For instance, television is a quick way to reach a large audience, but production costs are very high, and a message has to be brief. Brochures can provide in-depth information, but they take time to prepare and are expensive to distribute to a large audience. Public relations are considered very objective because your message is reported by an impartial third party, but you have little control over who will pick up your story.

- *Response.* It is not enough to choose the right vehicle and audience. Once the first steps are taken, follow-up, as will be discussed in detail in Chapter 5, is critical. Have enough people been given enough information to handle telephone inquiries adequately when the calls start coming in? If a free publication is promised in response to an ad, is the publication going to be ready to mail when requests start coming in?

Weaving the Elements into a Coordinated Plan.   A thorough plan for a marketing communications program is likely to consist of more than one vehicle. You should not plan for a brochure or an ad; your plan should be more—a campaign that can reach a particular audience for a particular purpose. This usually means having prepared follow-up or other complementary vehicles such as advertising during trade shows, sending direct mail out to support an advertising campaign, or following up direct mail with telemarketing. By doing this you ensure that your marketing materials gain leverage by supporting one another. At the same time, you have to be careful that your multiple media efforts support one another and do not make contradictory claims.

Balance is central in any campaign. You can balance short-term and long-term efforts in order to improve your image, sell your product or service, and ensure sound results. But remember that even though it is wise to balance exposure throughout the year, it is important to make sure that the greatest impact is created at critical decision-making periods. You must also be able to sustain efforts over time. For example, if you have decided to undertake an ongoing publication such as a newsletter, you must be sure to have enough material to keep it going. (If you don't have enough material, or if the content is thrown together because you lose interest over time, your publication will generate awareness—an awareness that is negative!)

On Budgets.   A critical part of your strategy is budgeting the right amount of money to carry out your marketing communications effort. No matter how tempted you may be to do so, don't develop the budget first and then build the plan around it. Decide what needs to be done to sell your service, and then match costs to needs, not needs to costs. Spend what is necessary to get the job done right. There is nothing to be gained from deciding on a $60,000 budget when $30,000 will suffice. Conversely, be careful not to decide to spend $30,000 when it takes $60,000 to produce the desired results. If you are worried about what management's reaction to the larger figure will be, think what the response to a failed effort, even if it costs little, will be.

Message

How does a strategy translate itself into a message? A good place to start is with the question: *If there is one impression that the vehicle must communicate to the audience, what is it?* If you keep the answer to this question clearly in mind, your message will be on target.

A Coordinated Effort. To get a message across forcefully, the entire marketing program has to achieve a unified effect. The style of the copy, the design, and even the paper stock are part of the message. These elements and others must be carefully coordinated so that they work together, not against one another. For example, you will destroy the effect of a brochure aimed at top executives if you create an elegantly written document with a sophisticated design—and then have it printed on inexpensive paper.

Similarly, individuals involved in a communications effort, such as the marketing manager, the designer, and the writer, should not compete to steal the show but should work together as a team. Their own personal goals have to be subordinated to the requirements of the product at hand. This can be accomplished with group brainstorming sessions and continual communication throughout the process. To do the best possible job, the writer and designer should have firsthand knowledge of and continuous access to the client, the service, and the industry. Only by knowing the audience can they keep its priorities clearly in mind.

Some Questions to Ask. Before writers actually sit down to write a message, they should be clear about certain parameters. These include the answers to the following questions.

- Can the message be explained in a few words, or does it require a long explanation? The answer to this question will help determine the style of writing and vehicle to choose. For instance, if it is necessary to educate a client because a service's benefits are not widely known, you would be better off with a seminar or personal contact than with direct mail. With direct mail, you are competing for the attention of the audience, and because the medium offers very limited space to express ideas, you will not be able to explain them in much detail.

- Should the message be conceptual or technical? This depends on the organizational level of the audience. Most top executives are likely to prefer an overview, while middle management might want more technical details.

- Should the message be personal or impersonal? Building a relationship is important in certain situations, such as when services are provided after a client buys a product. The personal trust you want to create will be destroyed by addressing a letter to "Dear Executive" instead of to a specific person, sending it bulk mail rather than first class, or placing a label on the envelope instead of typing it individually.

- Will the tone be hard-hitting or indirect? A hard sell might be effective in selling a book for $14.95, but it would not work in selling a plan to reorganize the structure of a company.

- How well does the audience understand the service and its benefits? If it does not understand the service, then education—rather than generating awareness, reinforcing a message, or selling to the audience—should be the primary objective.

- Will the material be seen with any of the firm's other communications materials? If so, it is important that the style, the appearance, and the messages of these materials be coordinated.

A Few Precautions. Buck Rodgers, a former vice president of worldwide marketing at IBM, once said, "People buy products for what they can do, not for what they are."[4] In other words, people do not buy products for all their features but for those benefits that specifically meet their particular needs. The better you address an audience's real needs, matching a product's benefits to an audience's requirements, the more effective the communication material will be. As simple as this sounds, it is often forgotten. It is easy to become so involved in the features of a product—or with the aspects of the product that the advertiser is most impressed with—that you lose sight of your audience.

Similarly, don't get caught up in words: Concentrate on meaning. The words you use must be so well aimed, must so clearly say exactly what you want them to and no more, that they inspire the desired behavior in your audience. Your words must inspire action—that is, interest in your service. Then, once the words are right, the style and design of your vehicle should work together to deliver them with just the right tone and emphasis. For example, if a client believes that services or products are too expensive, a very elaborate brochure will merely reinforce this fear.

The other important aspect of dealing with words is to be careful that you do not fall victim to overuse of jargon and buzzwords. They may impress colleagues and friends, but you are communicating the message to a lay audience, so it is necessary to speak their language. Technical jargon will confuse, not impress. Constantly using words that clients do not understand makes them feel confused, even inadequate. They respond to such language in the same way they would to a legal document permeated with incomprehensible terms—they stop reading it with care after the seventh page. Translate the message into language that the audience will understand and identify as their own.

Be careful also to look at *every* word you have written when you are finished to see if your message could be stated more clearly. The problem is so pervasive that IBM's house organ *Think* magazine recently began a new column, "Straight Talk," to call attention to it. The column presented a number of incredibly convoluted examples of how not to write:

One of the criteria indicated as determinant of who should be considered was regular participation at meetings. (In other words, let's pick the people who'll make most meetings.)

There is an existing problem which I would like to bring to your attention. It is a recurring one and one I feel is a hindrance to the project. (The suspense is killing us. What is it???)[5]

Executing the Plan

After spending so much time perfecting your marketing effort, you owe it to yourself—and to the communications campaign—to devote an appropriate amount of time to executing the plan. It is probably the most important element in your campaign. You can actually ruin the campaign with a lack of attention to details. For example, you must pay attention to details such as the temperature of a room and the way it is set up for a seminar, to the letter that accompanies a brochure, and to the mailing list that supports a direct mail program.

It is also important to coordinate your marketing efforts with those of other groups in the company to avoid duplication or, worse, to avoid showering the same audience with conflicting or mixed messages. Imagine how embarrassing it would be to send conflicting messages about your firm to subsidiaries of the same parent company. If you bombard people with many messages, you let them determine what is or isn't a priority; you thus lose control.

You must also be sure that all your firm's verbal and written communications convey the same message. Even though this is important in brief calls that are later followed by mailings, it is even more critical in visits where your firm's representatives leave materials behind after presentations. The materials left behind must reinforce—and in no way contradict—what the representatives have said.

There are a number of ways to monitor the results of your plan. You can develop a system to see whether direct mail is selling effectively on its own. You can observe how well follow-up is handled by keeping track of how many visits are made in response to queries and how quickly responses are made. You can also ensure that a corporate culture encourages responses and provides incentives for quick and effective follow-up.

An Emphasis on Quality and Substance.   Pay more attention to quality than to quantity. In sales efforts, only qualified leads deserve to be followed up, so be careful that every lead that comes along is not answered as a matter of course. Similarly, in public relations, it is much better to be mentioned in one major publication than in many less prominent ones. And, in planning any strategy, one good plan that is well executed beats many lesser plans that are not well executed.

Even a top-notch marketing communications program will not sell a product or a service that lacks substance; the service has to be worth selling. Although you can fool anyone initially, the emperor's new clothes made him the fool in the end. Selling empty promises is bad business.

Like most human endeavors, marketing communications is a process of constant growth. There are no formulas, shortcuts, or foolproof methods. The continuously changing environment calls for a constant process of evaluation and reevaluation: Is the program effective? Is it drawing the best rate of response? What are competitors doing? Most important, what can be done better than what is being done now? If you continue to probe and answer these questions as a matter of course, you are likely to begin to automatically build marketing communications campaigns with successful end results.

5

Direct Mail: Reaching the Right Audience with the Right Message

---

In a discussion of the problems inherent in advertising almost a century ago, retailer John Wanamaker said, "Half the money I spend on advertising is wasted; the trouble is, I don't know which half." You often hear the same words today. After all, general advertising is mass selling to broad groups, an activity similar to air-conditioning an entire building to keep its only two occupied units cool. Both do the job, but they do it inefficiently.

In contrast, direct mail targets the right audience with a message aimed directly at its needs. Remember that direct mail is a highly personal medium in which messages about your services and products can be customized. It is not restricted by time, like television or radio, or by the number of pages and format, like print advertising. It delivers an immediate call to action. Moreover, you can quantify the response to a direct mail campaign; it allows you to measure the impact of the dollars you have spent and to use that information to improve future performance.

In addition, direct mail has a multitude of applications. You can use it for soliciting new clients or orders; generating leads; creating a positive image that will aid future sales; cross-selling to existing clients; building brand loyalty, particularly when competing for a distributor's attention; increasing repeat orders; reactivating dormant accounts; increasing sales coverage; and servicing marginal accounts. Clearly, direct mail offers great opportunities. How you take advantage of those opportunities depends on your ability to execute the campaign. The six most common barriers to reaching the right audience with the right message are:

- *Putting Tactics Before Strategy.*   Failing to answer the broad questions of who you want to reach; how, when, and by whom decisions are made; which needs your service or product satisfies; how your competitors are positioning their services; and the market position you want to capture before creating your direct mail program are all costly mistakes. The questions you have to answer are similar to those every corporation's senior executives answer when deciding on the firm's goals. Every executive must decide not only what goals he or she wants to reach, but what the factors critical to achieving those goals are.

- *Overemphasis on the Creative Element.*   Treating the development of the list as an afterthought and ending up with a disorganized last-minute effort handled by low-level personnel who may not understand the importance of list strategy can make all the work done on the creative side pointless. All the artistry in the world will be wasted if it is merely admired by people who are in no way interested or in need of the service or product you are selling. The creative effort will also prove pointless if you know who you want to reach but the kinds of lists needed to reach those individuals are not available.

- *Impossible Deadlines.*   Three variables are involved in producing the package for the direct mail campaign: timing, quality, and cost. An overemphasis on any one of them comes at the expense of the others. The most common mistake is to set unrealistic deadlines. If you insist on getting it tomorrow, the costs will go up, and quality may go down.

- *Failure to Pay Attention to Details.*   Any failure to pay attention to even the smallest and most mundane detail when coordinating all the elements of the campaign can add to costs and reduce effectiveness.

- *Improper Follow-up.* Generating leads in such a way that they cannot be followed up promptly and professionally is worse than not generating any leads at all because it puts you in a poor position for future sales. In addition, you may generate business for a competitor by failing to follow up after making potential clients aware of a service or product.
- *Inability to Measure Program Effectiveness.* In developing a program that will generate leads, success is too often measured by the quantity rather than the quality of the leads produced. Leads that can't be followed up on or numerous leads from people who have no desire to buy are useless; what counts is the amount of business generated by the leads produced.

Reaching the Right Audience

At the heart of a direct mail campaign, assuming you are offering a useful service or a sound product, is the list. No matter how well you deliver your message, if you deliver it to the wrong audience, it is worthless. In fact, many experts claim that almost 50 percent of your efforts should be placed on list development.

First, it is essential to avoid becoming enamored of the size of the list when measuring the success of a mailing. In almost every case, the number of people who get your mailing has little to do with the response rate. A mediocre mailing sent to an excellent list almost always outperforms an excellent mailing sent to a mediocre list. For a $250-a-plate political dinner, a simple invitation sent to the 100 top contributors to the party in a given district will have a better response rate than a mailing of expensive invitations to all 5,000 voters in the same district. You can get the same number of attendees at a fraction of the cost.

Every company must decide how to go about obtaining lists. There are two basic sources for lists: internal databases and compiled lists purchased from outside. These sources should not be considered alternatives to each other. The most effective system merges all lists and always keeps them current and purged of duplicates. Every time you use a purchased list, every respondee should become part of your internal database.

Internal Databases

The beauty of an internal database is that you can load information from many sources and sort it any way you choose. A database can be built from records of past orders, past client lists, application forms, warranty cards, questionnaires and surveys, customer service reports, or requests for information and literature.

Database management is not a technical but a strategic issue. Output is more than stacks of names, labels, tapes, or printouts. Lists contain enormous amounts of information if they are well constructed and used correctly. In designing lists, your objective must be to divide the marketplace for your service into segments and then to choose those segments most likely to produce prospective clients. Properly coded, internal databases allow you to determine the buying characteristics of your clients—when was the last time they bought, how much they bought, how often they bought, which specific product or service they bought, and why they bought it. Moreover, your internal database not only allows you to target individuals but to target those who already have confidence in your firm and its services.

Compiled Lists

You probably could buy lists to reach almost every household and business in the United States. This might be useful in running political campaigns, where voter recognition of candidates is important, but it would defeat the usual uses of direct mail, where effectiveness depends on targeting. The more you can profile your present customers and find ones similar to them, the more likely you are to have a high response rate.

Recent advances in both technology and direct mail methods give you opportunities unheard of in the past. You can identify profitable prospects based on geographic, demographic, and psychographic characteristics and acquire lists accordingly. You can acquire business lists based, for example, on title, number of employees, sales size, zip codes, branch or headquarter location, and equipment owned. You can purchase consumer lists based on characteristics such as age, location, frequency of purchase, number in household, income, last purchase date, purchase patterns, and education.

No matter how good the lists you buy seem, you must set up a system that allows you to measure the response rate from them, noting which ones are most successful for future use. One simple, inexpensive method is coding return mail in such a way that you avoid excess print costs. For example, the department your return piece is addressed to can be typeset with a four-digit number, say, "Department 5678." If you are using four mailing lists, each with 1,000 names, a printer can be asked to scratch the last number off the plate after the first 1,000 are printed, another after the next 1,000, and so forth. By then matching the code on each piece returned to the list, you can determine which lists draw best. Because no major extra typesetting, platemaking, or printing are involved, there are no extra costs.

Presentation

Your mailings are always competing with other mail for time and attention. If you keep in mind that the U.S. Postal Service handled more than 58,238,290,000 pieces of direct mail in 1986, the magnitude of the challenge of making your presentation the one that attracts attention becomes clear. The scope of the problem was also pointed out in a study conducted by Stephan Direct, Inc., which reported that general managers, division heads, and presidents usually receive about 75 pieces of mail weekly, with some receiving as many as 200.[1] Thus, your package must be interesting enough to draw executives from their work. Your primary competition is every other piece of correspondence executives receive. Then, once you interest them in your service or product, your package must be attractive enough to make them pay more attention to it than to the mail they receive from your competitors.

There are any number of ways to look at the direct mail package that will go to your carefully targeted lists. In his book,

Successful Direct Marketing Methods, Bob Stone highlights many important aspects of the creative effort. He says that the "most effective mailing package consists of outer envelope, letter, circular, response form, and business reply envelope." He also highlights the importance of using indented paragraphs in the letter, of combining art and photography rather than using either alone, and of using two colors in letters. And he notes that third-class mailings pull as many responses as first-class mailings.[2]

These are not, however, meant to be rules. You can't guarantee future results based on past performance. Freeman Gosden said it best in *Direct Marketing Success:* "It is very difficult to guess response rates without testing . . . because there are too many factors at play. Price, uniqueness of product, competition's price, penetration of competition's advertising, ability to select lists, creative approach, guarantee statement, seasons, the image of the mailer and most important these days, economic conditions."[3] By offering specific benefits based on tested preferences, your message will be more persuasive and the response from it will be greater.

You can begin creative development by keeping in mind that your direct mail package is representing you to someone who cannot see you or your product. Your editorial, visual, and packaging take the place of feeling, seeing, touching, and even smelling your product or service. And they replace the enthusiasm projected by the inflections and speed of your voice and the excitement conveyed by your body language.

The direct mail package can use many devices to draw attention and maintain interest: an unusual medium (such as a cassette tape); art (such as children's drawings); die cuts (such as pop-ups); mailing process (such as an overnight courier); an unusual layout (a check or certificate); a three-dimensional item (helium balloons); special stock (giant letter); envelope design (such as one with a check showing through a window); shapes (such as a deck of cards with 52 messages with teaser copy).

A few of the components of the direct mail package are so critical to your success that they must receive the greatest part of the creative effort.

The Letter

In writing the letter, remember to have a specific image of a person in mind and write directly to that person, using language and mentioning benefits that mean something to that person. The letter, personalized if possible, must be easy to read, simple to understand, and arranged logically.

The opening paragraph should provide a promise to readers and avoid the obvious. The postscript, the paragraph most often read after the opening paragraph, should summarize the benefits and compel readers to act. Throughout, the copy should be in the active voice, use short sentences, substitute dashes for semicolons, and avoid unusual words that slow down readers. Keep in mind that specifics are more powerful than generalizations, that odd numbers are more believable than rounded ones, and that the letter should lead readers to the order form.

Personalization, one of the objectives of direct mail, can be accomplished by addressing the mailing using inkjet, computer-generated, or laser printers—or even by handwriting a message on the letter.

The design of the letter should be visually appealing to encourage readers to read on. This can be achieved by breaking up large blocks of copy, ensuring that the type is large enough to read and not too crowded on a page; in other words, make sure you plan for enough white space on each page. If you go on to a second page, break the last sentence on the first page in the middle to encourage readers to continue.

Sunbursts, headlines, captions, and postscripts will help with potential nonreaders; underlines, indents, bullets, bold type, and a second color will help those who skim.

Once the letter is completed, put it aside for a day, then try to answer the following questions.

- Does the letter create a sense of urgency?
- Do your claims, even when truthful, sound credible?
- Does the letter really say something, or is it merely a form letter?

- Does the letter make you want to respond?
- Does the copy wander, taking too long to make a point?
- Is your argument presented logically—written like a lawyer's summation to a jury, making the major points emphatically and convincingly?
- Is it necessary to read the whole letter before the offer is clear?
- Is the letter written in a style your readers are used to? For example, if the letter is intended to sell financial services to corporate executives, is the writing in it similar to that found in the *New York Times* or more like that in *People* magazine?
- Will the person and title at the end of the letter convey the image you want?

Writing

Writing is a critical element in every part of the direct mail package, not just in the letter. Clear, concise writing that is logical, interesting, and free of clichés will help sell your service or product. It gives the impression of a clear-headed, efficient, and well-organized company. It should have a tone of authority, but not pompousness; it should look professional, not amateurish. As Shell Alpert pointed out in *Business Marketing:*

> There is probably no more reliable indicator of amateurish copy writing than an inability or unwillingness to edit out redundant material and . . . using the same words over and over again. Take, for example, the powerful wonder word free. . . . Here are a few synonyms . . . complimentary, gratis, at our expense, without cost, gift, present, no-charge, gratuitous, bonus, award, prize, premium, dividend, reward, winnings, payout, payoff, prepaid, costless, guest sample, specimen, to keep, paid for by blank, benevolence, endowment, grant, trophy, memento, remembrance, largess, booty, stipend, commission, bequest, purse, token, souvenir, donation, keepsake, bounty, allowance, credit, on-the-house, no-payment due, yours for the asking, etc.[4]

It is also important to focus always on the needs of potential customers or clients when writing. In other words, telling readers that your product or service has a number of important features does not have the same impact as describing the benefits those features provide. For example, this book has a chapter on presentations. If that chapter were listed as a feature of this book in an advertisement, you would be less likely to want to read it than if the advertisement promises: "Make your presentations more exciting and appealing. Increase your persuasiveness in front of groups. Sell your ideas more effectively."

Typography

Typography is more than an art; it is another essential element in your direct mail packaging effort.

In a study of typographic design and its effects on communication, Colin Wheildon, a journalist and typographer, made a number of interesting observations that everyone involved in a direct mail package should keep in mind:

- 38 percent of readers showed poor comprehension when reading layouts which forced the eye to fight against reading gravity [the natural tendency of the eye to start at the top left corner of a page and move down to the right].
- 65 percent showed poor comprehension of articles set in sans serif body type.
- 72 percent showed poor comprehension of articles set ragged on the left.[5]

In addition, he notes that certain typographical elements, such as the overuse of capital letters, not only fail to encourage reading but actually discourage readers by throwing unnecessary distractions in their paths.

The overall use of design and layout affects readability too. Thus, it is important not to wait until the last minute to try to ensure that there will be time to study each piece in the package in final form before it is printed. For example, you may discover that a headline set just below the first two paragraphs of the text causes the reader to skip those paragraphs and read only what falls below the headline. Moving the headline to the top at this stage takes the pasteup artist a few minutes. Printing it the way it is, then realizing your error and being unable to do anything about it because the package is already late, may cost you potential clients.

The Offer

Human nature being what it is, procrastination or being afraid of making the wrong decision is natural. Once you have created a narrowly focused list of qualified prospects, a generous gift may be appropriate. Offers should be viewed as a variable cost, the objective being to increase response more than enough to offset the added costs of the offer. The gift might take the form of free information; it might be a limited offer or a complimentary sample; it might be a free trial or allow you to pay later.

On the other hand, a generous gift to an unqualified list will deluge you with leads to unqualified prospects. Leads that are too plentiful for your sales force to handle efficiently breed bad will, so be careful not to attract literature collectors, competitors, or students. As a general rule, the better the offer and the easier you make it to respond, the greater the response and the poorer the quality of the leads.

Reply Vehicles

A business reply envelope is essential if the response is confidential or if a check or credit card information will be enclosed with the order. It should have reminders—be sure your check is enclosed, has your address changed?—on the back to avoid wasted time. The business reply card should be positive, easy to fill out, reinforce the most important benefit, and create a call to action—and indicate what list the sender was on.

Scheduling

One barrier to successful direct mailing is an impossible deadline. The biggest problem with setting impossible deadlines for producing a package is additional cost. If you are running late, you will use more overnight carriers and messengers at every step of the production process. You will receive a large bill from the typesetter for author's alterations on errors discovered at the last minute. You will find that you cannot turn to the most economical printer because that company cannot turn out a job overnight; only specialty print houses that maintain 24-hour services—at substantial additional costs—can do so. You will discover that your postage bill is much higher than budgeted for because when you figured out the weight of the total package you forgot to include, for example, the response card.

An unrealistic schedule will also affect the program's impact. For example, calls on the offer that come before they can be handled properly or orders that arrive before the product is ready for shipment will cost you dearly.

Dedication to Detail

Every part of the direct mail campaign should be coordinated by someone who has the overall program clearly in mind. Responsibility for each aspect of the program should be assigned, and progress should be reported routinely. The details that must be taken care of vary from the critical to the mundane. For example:

- All the elements of the package must be well coordinated.
- All the ingredients of a continuing campaign must be woven together and take on a common look.
- To avoid boredom, avoid redundancy in message or design.
- Make a dummy of the package so that you can see all the elements the way your audience will. In addition to letting you see how the package holds together, the dummy also allows you to check such critical details as whether everything will fit in the envelope and the weight of the material before you commit to the purchase of stock for printing.
- Use seasons wisely. Coordinate your package with inventory and budgeting periods.
- Weigh the mailing. A one-ounce difference, not significant when mailing one piece, could prove very expensive when 80,000 pieces are involved.

- Check to see that your postal account is up-to-date and that your design conforms to postal regulations so that the Post Office will accept your reply cards.
- Call the phone number in the letter to see that it is correct and that your call is answered promptly.
- Make certain that mailings are properly coded for your database.
- Check to see that you are able to fulfill the offer.

Follow That Lead

Your direct mail program must include plans for following leads in a systematic and timely fashion. Your system must enable you to:

- Respond rapidly to an inquiry; that is, your people should have completed the training necessary to allow them to respond to new product inquiries and should have the information needed to distribute to respondents. Remember that for a lead tracking system to work properly, you must gain the cooperation of your sales staff. They must be made aware of the benefits that accrue from making the system work.
- Develop quality leads rather than numerous useless ones, such as leads resulting from too attractive a free offer for a simple response. Your response system must allow you to screen leads to determine which deserve priority. That will cut down on the number of initial turndowns during follow-up efforts, which will in turn build morale and make it easier to deal with the more elusive customers later on.
- Track the sales to see whether follow-up is taking place and whether leads are turning into orders or sitting in the top drawer of someone's desk. Where would your company fit into the following description of the lead tracking abilities of some major companies?

We went through September and October issues of nine different magazines and responded to every ad that offered literature. . . . Here's what actually happened.

Within one week 10 responses were received.

The second week, 42 replies were received.
The third week brought another 14 responses.
By the end of first month, we had heard from 11 advertisers.
Another month later, we heard from 11 more companies.
Four companies allowed three months to go by before responding.
Two more came in the fourth month.
One allowed five months to go by.
And, at the end of six months, five still hadn't responded.[6]

- Collect information for your internal database.

- Use it as a management tool, providing relevant information such as cost per lead and which marketing medium provides the greatest return. Which audience makes the best prospects? Which direct mail letters provide the greatest return? Which offers appeal most to your respondents?

Was It a Success?

When planning a direct mail campaign, look to the future. Be sure that you have incorporated methods of measuring how successful the campaign was and in what ways. You should be able to determine what percentage of increased sales is the result of the campaign. A system for identifying leads generated by the campaign, as opposed to responses to general advertising or word of mouth, is critical to future decision making.

The Lesson

Be careful not to become too enamored of any particular aspect of your operation. Remember that just as generals would not use their special tactical forces to fight every battle, direct mail by itself should not be expected to win every war. To achieve the greatest impact, direct mail must be coordinated with other elements to achieve an integrated marketing effort. The objective should be to utilize each medium for its inherent strength and deliver a timely message that is focused, consistent, and appealing to a targeted audience.

6

Networking: A World of Unlimited Resources

In dictionary terms, a network is a structure of cords and wires that cross at regular intervals and are knotted and secured at the crossings. Networking is the activity of creating networks. Unfortunately, *networking* has been so overused that it is no longer a clearly defined word but a "wordle"—a fictitious term used to describe a word or expression that is so overused that it has lost all meaning over time.

Today, people network by joining clubs, going to lunch with friends, attending conferences, joining industry associations, and going to alumni dinners and reunions: They network with church members, school buddies, community organizations. But what do these activities help them achieve in return for the time and effort they expend? Are the activities worth the investment? In other words, is there a right and a wrong way to network?

Those who know how to network swear by it. "Experienced networkers claim they can reach anyone in the world with only six interactions," says John Naisbitt in his book *Megatrends*.[1] Research identifying common characteristics of successful entrepreneurs notes that they "spent significant time developing new contacts and managing old ones (about 50 percent of the day)."[2]

Other people, though, treat networking as a game of business bumper cars: They show up at meetings two minutes before they start, they never contribute, and they do not spend the time needed to get to know people on a personal level. Instead, they measure their networking performance by the number of business cards that they manage to exchange as the meeting ends.

Those who network properly find that it provides many benefits. It serves as a source of information, new ideas, referrals, leads, new hires, market research, new service suggestions, and is a way to qualify or dispel rumors. On a personal level, networking can be a source of emotional support or career advice, it can help you find someone who can be objective about your business decisions, and it can be a source of long-term relationships. The possibilities are endless.

The Underlying Structure

According to the business literature, networking can be defined as:

> A pattern of human interactions characterized by a process of information exchange usually leading to other human interactions and/or material/service information, monetary or spiritual exchange.[3]

> An organized method of making links from the people you know to the people they know gaining and using an ever-expanding base of contacts.[4]

> The lines of communications, the alternative express highways that people use to get things done. In crisis and in opportunity, the word spreads quickly through these people—power lines.[5]

Networks are not formal groups operating under formal rules. They tend to be polycentric rather than monocentric, shaped like a spiderweb, where connections are made laterally, up and down, or across to other networks. Networks can be extensive or simple; the strength of the relationships among its members vary and are visible only to the individuals involved.

Networks are not hierarchical: No one is in charge, and the group does not depend on any single individual for its survival. Participation in networks is optional, and members treat one another as equals rather than as superiors or subordinates. Networks have no boundaries, formal agendas, or prescribed sets of rules; membership varies greatly as networks expand and contract at various times; and the life cycles of networks vary enormously.

A network is built on a foundation of mutual trust and support among members. Participants in a network come together because of common interests and objectives, and they voluntarily give of themselves (primarily through a barter system) because they know that by helping others they will eventually end up helping themselves. The people who join groups for personal gain but never contribute—who believe they are above the fray—are not really networking. They are takers, and other members of the group soon learn that they are not the people they want to network with.

You should limit your networking to groups that will help you achieve a goal you have set for yourself. As Casey Stengel once said, "If you don't know where you're going, you might end up somewhere else." Avoid joining organizations merely because they are prestigious groups whose names you want to place on your résumé. Becoming a member of such groups is wasted motion, not movement.

Ask yourself if you are networking for purely selfish reasons or whether you are prepared to give as much as you get. If you join a network to see what it can do for you, you may end up wasting your time—and the time of the other members. Before you begin networking, accept the fact that networks may not offer immediate rewards; they are resources for the future that require patience, commitment, and an investment from all their members.

Although it is often easier to tap into an existing network than to form your own, you should enter any network gingerly. It is best to join networks that are built around activities you enjoy and that consist of people who are giving and who believe networking involves two-way relationships. These can be found almost anywhere—at professional and trade associations, conferences, seminars and trade shows, software user groups, office parties, government groups, community organizations, and health clubs. Networks include business and school alumni, client contacts, vendors, airplane acquaintances, fellow commuters, parents of kids who go to school with yours, and family friends.

Some organizations can also assist you in your networking efforts, such as the National Organization of Women Business Owners of Chicago, the United Methodist Church, Pattern Research of Denver, Metasystems Design Group of Arlington, Va., and Strategic Connections Inc. of Denver.

Building Relationships

The relationships that develop during networking can be based on ties that are strong or weak. Give both types a chance. Don't decide "I'm the kind of person who only likes close associates" or "I'm the kind who doesn't like to be bound or confined by relationships," because both serve important purposes.

People you form strong ties with tend to be similar to you, so it is easier to ask them what they would do if they were you. They tend to travel in similar circles, so they hear what you hear and know who you know, which makes it easier for them to tell you how they would react in a similar situation. Moreover, they will be there whenever you need them and understand who you are and what makes you the person you are. None of these benefits accrues without an investment. People expect more time and effort from those they are close to, which means that you can develop only so many close ties.

Those you form looser ties with (for example, people from a different department in your firm or people you meet at seminars) are no less important than those you form stronger ties with, but they expect less of you. Weak ties allow you to obtain access to people of diverse backgrounds and specialty areas. They serve as bridges to other groups of people, provide greater objectivity in looking at your personal problems, and may approach a situation from an entirely different perspective than you would. They are the people you call and who call you for a quick discussion about the meaning of a development within your industry or those you introduce to your acquaintances at meetings and who introduce you to theirs. They may have very different backgrounds and experiences and travel in different circles. Therefore, they can provide insight or information that you or your associates do not have access to or may not have heard. The challenge is to know the benefits of both strong and weak relationships and to balance them carefully.

The other kind of balance required in networking is summed up best in *Corporate Networking* by Robert Mueller: "If we confine our networking only to those whom we know personally (or positionally) we miss the 'other world' out there of contacts and friends of our contacts and friends. This is the exciting, potential scope which networking offers when conducted in a conscious and determined way."[6]

Turning Talk into Action

The first step in properly utilizing a network is to identify and document the personal strengths of its members. Discover all you can about them. Learn whether they have influence, can generate or evaluate new ideas, can serve as a source of competitive intelligence, can alert you to new business opportunities, can help you with personal problems, have good business acumen, are likely to know what's happening in XYZ Corporation, have good contacts to refer you to, know good sources of information, and have an excellent knowledge of business fundamentals.

The next step is to divide the members of your network into categories so that you can easily determine which people to call when you need assistance. For example, decide who is good with details and who sees things well in conceptual terms. Who has experience in a large bureaucracy or with an entrepreneurial unit? Who has experience working with the government, with non-profit organizations, or family-run businesses? Who has had experience with a business going through extraordinary growth, a turnaround, downsizing, or a merger or hostile takeover? Who will be honest with you when you need it or will hold back to avoid hurting your feelings?

The final step is to identify your own personal strengths and to determine in what ways you can help others achieve their personal goals. After all, networking is a two-way street. People who begin by asking how they can be successful, effective, and happy solely within themselves are making a fundamental error. Rewards and successes go to those who have learned to trust others, are willing to provide others with assistance, and recognize the rights of others to make demands on them. Any attempts you make at networking will fail if you offer little and always ask for a lot.[7] If you consciously look for ways to help others without expecting anything in return, you can look forward to the day when you will be on the receiving end.

Networking: An Activity with a Purpose

As Regis McKenna, author of *The Regis Touch,* once said, "Word of mouth is probably the most powerful form of communication in the business world. . . . Word of mouth is so obvious a communications medium that most people do not take the time to analyze or understand its structure. To many people, it is like the weather. Sure, it's important. But, you can't do much about it. You never see a Word-of-Mouth Communication Section in marketing plans."[8] What McKenna is discussing is the failure to give networking the priority it deserves and the opportunities you miss as a result of that failure.

From a marketing perspective, networking can be useful in seven different ways:

- It can provide *knowledge* by allowing you to study, through network members, successful organizations and individuals and to learn from them.

- It can provide you with *resources,* for example, by gaining you access to good recruits, new suppliers, and better equipment.

- It allows you to *position* your organization favorably by influencing those who influence the decision makers you deal with. This will have a long-term impact on your sales.

- It can be used to create *opportunities* to place your organization in the right place at the right time.

- It provides *referrals* to others who need your products and services.

- It can help you *solidify existing relationships,* improving your chances to cross-sell.

- It allows others to provide you with *leads,* making it possible for you to be everywhere at once.

These opportunities are worth further examination.

Knowledge

Networking provides much more than the short-term gains traditionally associated with new business leads or referrals. You must understand that you do not know it all and that you can learn from the experiences and successes of others. That attitude enables you to gain knowledge (from those within or outside your industry) that you can then apply to your organization. The key is not being defensive about what you do not know: Ask questions and listen to others.

A good example was described in the *Wall Street Journal* not long ago:

> Networking is becoming something more like what happened to Chris Hoezle, owner of a Santa Ana, California, computer-products company. Back in 1986, his company was "within inches of failing," as he puts it. While attending several discussion sessions for executives on how to improve management techniques, sponsored by the American Electronics Association, he got to know a business owner who had weathered the same kind of crisis and came through it a spectacular success. Mr. Hoezle was invited to spend an afternoon touring his fellow executive's organization and reviewing the key elements of his turnaround. He received insights on eliminating certain fixed expenses, reducing staff, and reorganizing for efficiency. Mr. Hoezle's revenues have since tripled, with a staff one-third the size it was in 1966.[9]

Resources

Networking is an excellent way to gain access to resources that might otherwise be hard to find. For example, how often have you heard someone on the 5:45 train say, "I just lost a technical writer on my staff. Do you know a writer with a background in manufacturing technology who might be interested in such a position?" or "I was thinking of making the switch you did to internal production of our newsletters. What equipment did you buy?" or "I'm just not happy with one of our suppliers. Where do you get your ink?" or "I know you just left XYZ Corporation to join MNO Corporation last month. Well, we're making a presentation to XYZ, and I can use any background material you could give me on them."

In an article in the *Washington Post,* the president of BDM International Inc. and the former director of the American Cancer Society's northern Virginia chapter, says that "executives of high technology companies tend to gravitate to charities with some connection to education because of a growing concern over the shortage of engineers, scientists, mathematicians and qualified technicians needed in the high tech field. Such a direct connection between the charity and the corporate interest, [he] said, makes it easier for executives to justify the time they spend on charity work."[10] The value of networking as a way to tap into resources is clear at the highest corporate levels.

Positioning

Networking is an indirect strategy that allows you to position your organization favorably by influencing those who influence the decision-making process. As Regis McKenna said, "I believe that 10% of the people in an industry influence the other 90%. If a company can win the hearts and minds of the most important 10% its market position is assured."[11]

One of the ways to use networking for positioning is to win an endorsement that carries weight. Such an endorsement can come, for example, from an important business adviser (a noted banker, accountant, attorney, consultant), an influential client, a respected Wall Street analyst, a widely read publication, a well-known reporter, a leading figure in the corporate world, a trade association, a politician, or an academic researcher. The question is, how do you go about getting that endorsement?

First, decide exactly what audience you wish to influence—the decision makers of individual companies, an industry group you want to penetrate, or consultants to *Fortune 500* companies. Next determine how members of such groups are influenced. Who are the people they listen to? Which individuals and groups have the greatest credibility with them? Who are the members of their inner circle? Which publications do they read most often?

Now you must figure out how your network can help you reach the people your potential clients listen to. Before asking for introductions, be sure you know whether someone in your organization has been in touch with these people in the past and if you or your organization is a known commodity. If you are known, how are you perceived? Is their image of you very different from what you would like it to be? If it is, you must find a way to change that image. Unknown? You must get information to them to begin building that image. Someone in your network may be able to provide you with that all-important introduction to them. Then you can begin by introducing them to your organization, provide an exclusive look at a new product, provide a glimpse of future products, or educate them on a proprietary technology.

Opportunity

How can you best use networking to position yourself or your organization favorably so that you can take advantage of being in the right place at the right time? The concept is simple. If you provide services to manufacturers, you could serve as keynote speaker at a manufacturing conference (demonstrating your expertise among your buying audience), publish an article in a manufacturing industry publication (which will probably be circulated), or become active in a manufacturing association. By doing any of these things, you increase the likelihood of meeting people who can assist you in your personal or business efforts.

The *Washington Post* said, "Other executives say they also pick the charities with which they get involved with an eye toward helping causes that are complementary with their business. For some guys it's almost a science. They choose charities with high recognition or good penetration into the business sectors they're involved in, said a top executive at a Fairfax high-technology firm."[12]

One word of caution, though: I have found that people who speak at conferences, write articles, and join associations for the sole purpose of selling turn off their audience. You must first provide value to the audience without any expectation of receiving benefits.

Referrals

Another benefit of networking is referrals. These come in many forms, from many sources, and involve many different levels of participation by the person serving as the referral.

The first kind of referral is a result of performing work for a respected individual or company. At a later date, in the course of a business presentation, the mere fact that you casually drop someone's name as a client in the course of the discussion, without giving any details, leads your potential client to think, "If it was good enough for them, it's good enough for me." Your initial client may not even know about the discussion, but it does not matter because you did no more than mention that he or she was a client, without providing details or attributing any opinions to him or her. This is the kind of referral that requires no participation from the person providing it.

Another kind of referral involves using, with a firm's or an individual's agreement, a name to endorse your product or service. The most common forms are book or seminar endorsements. These require minimal participation—at most, writing the endorsement.

Yet another form of referral is a reference from a satisfied client. It can take the form of a list of colleagues within or outside an organization who may be interested in your product or service. It may be granting permission for you to use a name to gain entrée (and agreement to stand as a reference if necessary) or to stand in support of you if you need a reference for a potential client.

There are two other important forms of referral. The first consists of comments made about someone in front of a large group. Anyone present who currently needs the services of the person mentioned or may need them in the future will remember what was said. The second is the most active form, usually seen in politics, where an individual, such as a member of Congress, aggressively speaks out on behalf of another party.

Keep in mind some basic rules when using someone as a referral:

1. Never use people's names without first securing their permission. Even if they are close friends, the organization where they work may prohibit it.

2. If you are given the name of someone to call (a referral), it is professional courtesy to keep the initial contact informed of any actions that you take or results that occur.

3. People who allow you to use their names do so only because they assume you will provide the same or better service to the person they refer you to than the service they were receiving and that you will make them look good. (If you do not, you may destroy two relationships in the process: The client will stop using you, and the person who put his or her reputation on the line for you will be angry and disappointed.)

4. Never take someone's good nature for granted; a thank-you is required.

5. Lastly, when asking people to speak on your behalf, make sure that you either know what they are going to say or that you adequately prepare them with information to use.

Solidifying Existing Relationships

Networking can solidify existing relationships. People good at handling their clients usually spend so much time with them and become so intertwined in their businesses that they seem like full-time employees of those clients.

Once you become part of clients' inner circles, you can discover any number of things that will help you build stronger relationships with your clients and develop new opportunities to market your services. You can learn where and why clients are using your products and services and whether they are using them properly. The latter is particularly important: If, for example, you provide market research information, and your clients are not using that information to address their business problems, they will be less likely to call you in the future.

Once you realize what is happening, you can make sure that the service you provide is more effectively used. You also will discover what new services clients need that your firm might be able to provide or be able to develop, especially if they would be useful to other clients as well. You will also have a chance to respond to questions or to small problems before they become large, and you will learn early on whether competitors are making inroads with your clients. Once you have shown that you are a caring person, if the client contact should leave that company, not only will he or she see to it that a replacement knows about you, but the relationship with him or her will continue. All of the concern and help you provide—not just because you are trying to make additional sales—will result in close personal relationships that will transcend the business relationship.

Leads

The final benefit of networking is also the most obvious: It is a source of leads, of people who will, on your behalf, watch out for new business opportunities and then alert you to them. For example, a real estate agent will call a friend—a local banker—before a new family moves into town (providing the banker with an opportunity to gain a new account). An interior designer, office construction worker, or building manager will alert friends in, say, an office products company of a new firm moving into town. An accountant may give a referral to an investment professional, a consultant to the seller of computer hardware, an architect to a builder. The possibilities are endless.

Why Doesn't Everyone Network?

If networking provides all these benefits, why doesn't everyone network?

Personal Barriers

Many people are uncomfortable reaching out to others or cannot believe that there is value in doing so. They may believe that it is always better to depend on themselves because they have not learned to trust others. The major personal barriers to networking usually fall into one of the following categories.

Selfishness. Some people do not believe they need anyone's help or advice. They also do not believe that it will be worth their while to extend themselves ("He could never give me information worth the time it will take me to help him"). If they cannot see an immediate reward, such individuals will not join a network.

Myopia. Some people are so shortsighted that they are unable to comprehend the value of networking or foresee the need for it. Because they do not see ahead, they accept their own conviction that they are too busy today to network, and they know they will never find the time tomorrow.

Shyness. Some people just find it too uncomfortable or difficult to approach those they do not know. They prefer to stay in the background and always let others make the first approach. Basically, they hate to leave the comfort zone and deal with anything unfamiliar.

Lack of Know-How. Some people just do not know the benefits of networking, how to take the first step, or how to find a network to join.

Missing Work Ethic. People who never feel compelled to produce the best or the most can see no value in networking. So long as they do just enough to keep a job, they are satisfied.

Networking Is Not an Extracurricular Activity

The second barrier to networking is being part of an organization that discourages it. In such an organization, even if you are able to overcome your hesitation and reach out or if you enjoy meeting new people, asking questions, and opening up, you may find that your firm's culture does not support networking.

In such a firm, an announcement that you want to attend an out-of-town meeting of people in your field is greeted as a request for a free vacation. If you are allowed to go, you find yourself being given instructions that will make it impossible for you to network comfortably: Find out what you can about our competitors, but be careful what you say. Another all-too-famil-iar reaction is the one many people who ask permission to attend a seminar get—"Don't you have any work to do?"

If this is a problem in your organization, you can change this attitude in a number of ways. First, do all the networking you can on your own time. Be friendly with fellow commuters, attend town meetings, join clubs, manage a Little League team. Then, whenever the networking process benefits your organization, let management know about it. Even if you never convince manage-ment of the value of networking, you may find the perfect con-tact to help you make the next move up the career ladder—with an organization that values networking.

How Can You Make Networking Work?

Networking is a long-term strategy. Networks improve con-stantly over time as they are shaped and molded by their staunchest members. To be part of a successful network you must follow a few rules.

1. Don't wait until you desperately need a network to begin developing one. Networks are based on trust, respect, and personal chemistry; they are not developed overnight.

2. Become active in organizations; don't just grace everyone with your presence. Be selective in choosing the group that you participate in. There are no shortcuts to getting in-volved: You receive only as much as you are willing to give.

3. Remember that seminars, conferences, and committee meet-ings are not substitutes for one-on-one meetings. In group meetings, some members are intimidated and suppress their opinions. Because large meetings tend to have set agendas that remain the focus of discussion throughout, it may be difficult to get members to focus on anyone's personal situa-tion. Moreover, in large groups a few members may domi-nate discussions. In addition, there may be people present at the meeting whom you can't discuss your situation in front of.

4. Collecting a lot of business cards and then wrapping them up in a rubber band, only to collect dust, isn't networking.

5. Remember that because successful networks change and evolve, expand and contract, they must be continually nurtured by all their members. Therefore, you must keep in touch with members of your network.

Some Rules for Ensuring Success

Use Caution at the Outset. In order to establish a relationship, you often have to make the first move. But it is important that your initial gesture be something other than a request. For example, sending promotional literature out as an initial overture is not networking—it is selling. Earlier I discussed the importance of knowing the strengths of your network members. Well, the other half of that equation is knowing their personal needs as well. If they do not find some way of using the network to satisfy themselves, they will be far less likely to participate. The way to ensure that you do something to help meet their needs is to listen to what they say from their perspective rather than filtering the information through your biases.

Be Prepared. Keep in mind that you are not likely to be of any help to people in your network if you have information that ties in with a problem they need solved but can't seem to place your finger on it. Part of the investment that you must make is to organize yourself so that you are in a better position to help others. One way to do this is to use cards or a computer listing of those you network with to record information that might be of use to them when you hear it.

Find the Right Approach. When you decide you really need the help of your network, you have to decide which member to approach with your request and how to make the request. Once you know exactly what you need, it is easier to decide who is best able to field the request. If timing is not critical, you can ask a number of members for help, and you can ask them to ask their contacts for help as well. Also, when making a request, do not always seek the obvious. Based on categories you established earlier, you may get five different answers (or perspectives) on the same issue. For example, a writer I know sends a manuscript out to be read by as many as five people—an expert in the subject area, an editor to review it for grammar and style, someone unconnected with the field to determine how clearly the material is presented, someone representative of the target audience to be sure it contains information of interest, and a member of his own organization to check for internal political sensitivity.

Avoid Mistakes.   There are many ways to become an unpopular member of a network. Although most people generally like to help others and give advice—when you ask for help, you pay the person you ask a compliment—remember that they like to be approached gradually and not be put under pressure. Be careful to assess carefully the ability of the person you plan to ask. If you rush out and ask people to respond to requests without thinking about their ability to respond, you may embarrass them by forcing them to admit they cannot help.

Use other people's time wisely. Know what you want before making a request. Too many people pick up the phone and call before they decide exactly what they need. The result is a long call that helps you focus on what you need, but because it becomes clear that the person you called is obviously not the right person to help you, you are both embarrassed.

Evaluate the reasonableness of your requests. Are you asking people to put their necks on the line? Will it cost them a lot of time and money? Would you do it for them if the tables were turned?

Respect other people's priorities. Your requests may be priorities and may not seem to be major undertakings to you, but the people you ask may have a full plate at the moment, which means that, much as they would like to help you, they cannot find the time to do so.

Be specific in your requests. If you are vague, you may end up getting something that you don't need. Tell the people you call why you need what you asked for, and ask them how they would approach the same problem. This allows them to be creative; moreover, they very well might have a different perspective or approach the situation from an angle you have not yet explored.

Also, be sure you explain what has been done to date so that they don't spend valuable time and effort duplicating someone else's efforts.

Pattern Research, a networking organization, has provided examples in their membership manual of the wrong and right ways to ask for something:

> Wrong ways to ask a favor:
> "I am dropping off 50 copies of my 110 page business proposal for you to mail out . . ."
> "Are there any people in your network looking for a smart investment deal?"
>
> The right ways to ask the same favor:
> "If I wanted to distribute my business plan to some interested network users, how should I handle it?"
> "I have a high risk real estate deal for people looking for a legal tax shelter. The minimum investment is just $5,000."[13]

Reciprocate. When you are approached with a request, keep in mind that if you can't fulfill it, the next best alternative is to recommend someone who might be able to.

Networking Protocol

Networking should not be a haphazard, on-and-off affair. To network successfully, you would be wise to read over the following protocol and keep it handy for review.

- Networking must be a give-and-take relationship. If you do too much for a person without ever accepting something in return you end up making the recipient hesitant to ask for more and imply that he or she has nothing to offer.
- Give and take is not done on a one-for-one basis. Just because you have performed one favor does not mean you should expect one in return. Gaining a reputation as someone who keeps score, who is always looking for a quid pro quo, will make future networking harder.
- When you do someone a favor, do it without making a big deal out of it. Either do it because you want to help, or don't do it. Be sure not to act as if you expect something in return.

- Besides giving what is asked for, another way of providing value in a relationship is to suggest you can do more when you think you might have something additional to offer. Don't, however, give something extra without asking. This is a lot like giving a gift: You should give people what you know they want, not what you want them to have.

- Do not provide assistance that has not been asked for, and do not push yourself on people. You might mean well, but you will be guilty of the business equivalent of what happens when a child with a new pet kitten holds it so tightly it smothers.

- Do not try to show off and answer a question by telling everything you know about a subject or by sending people 15 volumes of material when one article that sums it all up would suffice. They will be annoyed when they realize they have wasted valuable time. Information overload is bad business, and quality is always preferable to quantity.

- Do not make promises you can't deliver. It is better to say you can't do something immediately than to have someone depend on you for something you cannot deliver until it is too late for him or her to do anything about it.

- Make sure your calls are convenient. Clients may be in meetings or may be working on critical projects that have to be ready that afternoon. Also, some people prefer to be called at the office, others at home. Be conscious of their desires.

- Try not to become too reliant on any individual. You can destroy the best of relationships by relying too much on someone and by taking advantage of that person.

- When making requests of others, be considerate. Do not request sensitive information, watch the costs of your requests in time and money, and make sure your requests are ethical and reasonable.

- When people come to you with problems they have labored over for weeks, the last thing they want is for you to solve it for them in seconds. If you do so, you suggest that they have overlooked the obvious and are stupid. One way to avoid this is to ask questions that lead them to solve the problems themselves.

- Sensitive information should not be shared with anyone else. If you do so and those who provided the information find out, you will lose their trust. What's more, the person to whom you relayed that information will know you cannot be trusted—him today, me tomorrow.

- Avoid divulging or asking people to divulge sensitive information or information their organization considers to be confidential.

- Do not judge other people's requests. What might seem foolish to you may be a priority to them for reasons they are hesitant to reveal.

Conclusion

If you make networking a part of your life, you will soon find yourself part of a larger, richer world filled with new relationships, new opportunities, and vast resources. It will be a world in which you will constantly meet new people who you enjoy and admire, people who can learn from you and people you can learn from, people who enjoy sharing and giving and are willing to lend an ear when things are going wrong or pat you on the back when they are going right. They will be people you take enormous pleasure and satisfaction in helping, knowing that you are all becoming part of a rich circle of people involved with and committed to one another.

7

Relationship Management: More Than Wining and Dining

In the halls of every organization, the same frustrations can be heard:

- "Our sales costs are skyrocketing: How can we make our marketing dollars go further?"
- "Our competitors keep beating us to market with new services: What can we do to get there first?"
- "Two of our employees called on the same client and made contradictory claims: How can we keep such mistakes from happening?"

Each of these seemingly unrelated problems can be resolved in the same way: relationship management. Relationship management can stretch marketing dollars by curtailing the need to search constantly for new clients; it can keep a firm aware of its clients' needs for new services; and it can stop the erosion of its existing client base. What it takes is focusing the efforts and resources of everyone involved in selling the service to those few potential or existing clients that offer the best business opportunities. Relationship management assumes that a sale is not a one-time event but part of an ongoing relationship between seller and buyer that requires the seller to make a commitment to the buyer—in the expectation that the effort will be reciprocated.

Your key to managing ongoing relationships is careful client planning. Such planning involves more than taking someone out to an expensive lunch or to a ballgame on a Saturday; it requires more than just a friendly telephone call every two or three weeks. These tactics can be useful opening gambits to get your offer a hearing and then to help you to maintain a personal relationship and build trust between you and your client. But the goodwill these tactics create soon fades if you do not live up to the promises you made, if the quality of the service your organization provides is not good, if you do not deliver on your promises, or if competitors offer new and better services.

Ongoing Sales Relationships Versus One-time Sales

More is expected in an ongoing sales relationship than in a one-time sale. For example, when it comes to a one-time purchase of a product like a camera, your customer will examine the features of various products, compare prices, and consider the salesperson's performance and the dealer's reputation. When it comes to hiring an investment consultant, a client will ask about potential consultants' backgrounds, their track records and investment philosophies, whether they keep current on the latest tax laws, the quality of their research departments, whether their company is in good financial health, and will ask if they can call existing clients to ask for references. In an ongoing sales relationship, the stakes are raised, and new criteria are added. Buyers of expensive telecommunications equipment or corporations that want to be sure they can integrate their systems need some assurance that sellers will remain in business and be leaders in the field, that they are committed to the technology and the product, and that they devote enough resources to research and development to be able to update and improve their services and provide new services in the future.

In addition, buyers want assurance that sellers have and will continue to maintain high-quality services and can serve their needs consistently in many locations. But perhaps most important to buyers is a sense that sellers have the will and commitment to build ongoing relationships and that the sellers' capabilities will keep up with theirs.

A "Win-Win" Situation

Developing an ongoing relationship benefits both buyers and sellers. By focusing all their resources on organizations that promise the greatest long-term returns, sellers can maximize marketing efforts while serving buyers' best interests.

For the Seller

Once the relationship is under way, the emphasis for sellers should shift from a selling to an advisory role. They should look for ways to help clients and observe their operations to determine if there are additional needs they can fill. Sellers emphasis should shift from the one-time sale to providing real value to buyers, from continually searching for new prospects in many firms to building ongoing relationships in a few. Remember that the better you understand the needs of your client, the stronger the relationship will be.

Buyers and sellers can work together to modify and improve current services and to develop new ones. When that happens, buyers become excellent sources of new ideas, helping sellers to test new products, providing information about the way services are used, and suggesting ways to improve them. Of course, buyers involved in developing a service will be much more enthusiastic about using it once it is available. Norman Wholley, vice president of corporate markets of what was then called American Can, once said, "If we do not have something for you in our laboratories, something is missing from the relationship."[1]

With an ongoing sales relationship, buyers can grow as sellers grow. Sales can increase exponentially by cross-selling (see Chapter 12) or by marketing throughout buyers' organizations—horizontally into other functional areas; vertically to those on higher or lower hierarchical levels; and to other locations, divisions, subsidiaries, or product areas. Of course, opportunities for cross-selling must be exploited deliberately, as a matter of policy. To be effective, cross-selling requires not only support from management and a workable organizational structure but a frame of mind that regards every sale or transaction as the beginning of a new sales opportunity, not the culmination of an old one.

For the Buyer

When sellers are better acquainted with buyers' organizations and industries, buyers will get better product performance. Services will, over time, be tailored more specifically to their needs, and sellers will begin to coordinate their organizations' efforts to meet future needs. Once buyers and sellers have built an ongoing relationship, buyers will have fewer surprises, will have smoother product transitions, and will deal with the same people all the time. If all goes well, all levels of both organizations will become involved in and committed to the relationship. Frequent communication will increase the amount of trust in the relationship and, by keeping management in both organizations informed about situations and about each other, allow for quicker decision making.

How to Begin

Former Union Carbide chairman Warren Anderson once said, "Now we are measuring the success of our selling efforts not only in terms of volume of business but in . . . planned growth of business with individual customers over the years."[2]

"Planned growth of business with individual customers" is the result. The question is, how do you get there? Two approaches are possible. The first is to concentrate on current accounts. Such a concentration fits the 80/20 rule: When 20 percent of your clients provide 80 percent of your business, they warrant special attention. The second approach is to focus attention on a few nonclients who provide real potential—that is, narrow your marketing effort from broad-based marketing to focus on those few nonclients who seem like potential long-term clients.

Once new business targets have been chosen, your real work begins. Keep in mind that all the research into potential clients will be in vain if, as soon as such possibilities are identified, your employees charge out the door unprepared. It is critical that everyone involved in the sales effort know everything about the firm they represent, the competition, and the client.

Researching Your Firm

Knowing your firm sounds so obvious that it is often overlooked. Does your firm have the resources to serve a potential client well? Depending on your service, resources might include product specialists, industry specialists, administrative support, and those who can interact with clients around the country or around the world. Not having such support can be as dangerous to your sales effort as is the general with all the troops and weaponry he needs to launch a siege against a city some 100 miles away failing to ensure that his supply masters will be able to provide food and water to support troops.

It is also important to look at your services to decide exactly which will be most beneficial to your particular client. This includes not only the services you are personally familiar with, but all of your organization's offerings. In discussing one service, clients might ask you about another that they have heard about but that you are not very familiar with. It is not important to be an expert in every area. It is important, however, to be able to identify potential opportunities, to be able to converse on a subject, and then to be able to bring in a colleague who is an expert. Know what services have been sold to other firms in the buyer's industry, what service applications have benefited those firms that might be useful to your new client, and be able to capitalize on the knowledge that you've gained about failures with similar companies so they can be prevented in the future.

Researching the Competition

It is important that you look not only at actual competition but also at potential competitors who would present a real threat if they pursued a client. For example, 15 years ago General Motors viewed Ford and Chrysler as archenemies; no one imagined that the Japanese would make the inroads into the automobile market that they have.

A 1989 survey of 315 companies by the Conference Board noted that "competitive intelligence programs have at least five major objectives:

- avoid surprises
- identify threats and opportunities
- gain competitive advantage by decreasing reaction time
- improve planning
- help managers and executives better understand their own companies."[3]

There are many ways to achieve these five objectives. For example, you can find out what inroads competitors have made with a client and its subsidiaries at its various locations. What did the client see in those competitors? If you can answer that question, you will have insight into the client's priorities. Why has the client now decided to talk to you? Your competition must be failing to fulfill some need. You can learn a great deal from a competitor's successes and failures. You must also be aware of any personal alliances between a client and the competition and of any situations in which bridges have been burned. For example, did the competition promise prompt service and not deliver? If that is the case, you will find it very useful to stress your service department's record and to suggest that the potential client talk to another client who has had particularly good experiences with the department. Knowing all you can about your competitor's weaknesses, for example, bureaucratic structure, lack of personal attention, inconsistent service delivery, weak offices, turnover, narrow geographic coverage, and so forth, can all be useful in planning your presentation. In addition, knowing how your competitor's employees are compensated (for bringing in new business as opposed to maintaining the existing client base, for performing services, for cross-selling) may make it possible to anticipate an action.

Researching the Buyer

Most important of all, perhaps, is your knowledge of your client's organization, its history, its divisions, and its locations. A study of client satisfaction reported that almost 40 percent of bank customers "said that their bankers barely understand their business or don't understand it at all. Only 14 percent said bank officials understand their business 'very well,' while the rest said the bankers understand it moderately well."[4] That is why it is so important to look at your client's business from all angles, including which of its services are most and least profitable and how it differentiates itself from its competition. Find out who the firm's decision makers are and the issues that senior management is confronting. Consider the firm's relationships with other vendors, and study any past relationships between the firm and your own organization. Collecting this kind of information requires research. Examine annual reports, speeches, and references to the company in periodicals and newspapers. Talk to as many of its former and present employees, clients, and competitors as you can. If it is a public company, you might even talk to a stockbroker about it. Be sure you know:

- How decisions are made in the organization. (For a more detailed discussion of this, including how to decide who has influence, whether decisions are made by an individual or a committee, and what financial criteria must be met, see Chapter 8.)
- If the organization has established buying criteria.
- If the service will be considered a commodity or a strategic element in the client's business.
- What the client's past relationships with other vendors were like, how the client first learned about your firm, and what brought the client to call you.
- If the organization currently uses another of your firm's services; if they do take full advantage of that service?
- If the client ever used your firm's services in the past; if it no longer does, find out what happened.

Anticipating Obstacles

After you have done your research, the next step is to survey possible obstacles that could surface during your first meeting. Once you do, develop a presentation that addresses the objections before they are stated. It is, after all, much easier to walk through a mine field when you know where the mines have been placed.

In your presentation, take into consideration what capital investments have already been made and what changes would be required to use your service. Who was included in making the decision that may be unmade? What were some of the criteria used in making the previous decision? What would your service mean to people in the organization? Would it replace some people? Is training necessary? Are your products and services and the benefits they provide understandable, tangible, measurable? If not, what can you do to make them more so? How would a decision to buy your service affect those responsible for the current situation? If it is likely to reflect unfavorably on them, what kinds of obstacles are they likely to put in your path—for example, during implementation of your service?

Strategies for Starting a Relationship

In general, you should keep four basic strategies in mind when trying to penetrate a new account or to expand your sales effort within an existing account.

Minimize Resistance.   Avoid direct confrontation with the competition, and, at the same time, minimize potential resistance from a buyer. One way to do this is to start a relationship in an area without strategic significance for the customer or for the competition. For instance, enter an industrial account by providing maintenance, spare parts, or low-margin accessories. In the service sector, a law firm with special expertise in copyright law might begin its approach by offering services to a corporation's communications division. By keeping a low profile, you can postpone any retaliatory efforts from the competition, perhaps until it is too late for them to stop your inroads into an organization. The important thing at the start is to get your foot in the door, to get to know the people, and to build confidence before entering the market in force.

An interesting example of this kind of effort involves Nintendo, the game maker that entered 21 percent of all U.S. households with a harmless toy. Low-end computer manufacturers interested in selling their machines as a means of interacting with shopping and banking services have discovered that the toy was a Trojan horse. Now, in Nintendo, they have a new competitor who will soon be marketing software that allows its hardware to perform numerous additional functions. The game maker never announced the possibilities; it just went out and captured an enormous market share before its competitors knew what was happening.[5]

Find Out Where the Competition Is Vulnerable. Timing is a critical element in any strategy. For example, a client will be more apt to consider a new service when the competition is changing its model or introducing a new technology. At that point, the potential client is open to change. Indeed, holding onto existing clients through such changes has proved a severe problem for many computer companies. According to Kenneth H. Olsen, Digital Equipment's president, after years of promoting a specific computer design, changing to new products "confused our customers, and it hurt us."[6]

Another good time to try to get a foot in the door is when a new person has been promoted or hired as a decision maker or when someone has been added to the decision-making process. This is a perfect opportunity if you have previously encountered resistance in trying to penetrate that account: The new person is unlikely to be aware of the past difficulty and is thus likely to grant you a hearing. Also, the alliance that may have existed with the previous buyer is no longer a concern.

Wherever possible, you should take advantage of your competition's weaknesses. For example, your chances of selling your service to a client who has always dealt with a competitor's star salesperson improves when that person leaves or gets promoted. Since the client's comfortable relationship is no longer in place, getting a foot in the door is far easier.

You can also capitalize on such situations as a competitor's failure to provide adequate service or follow-through, its neglect of a secondary market, or its wrongheaded or desperate attempt to make a sale that is not in a client's best interest. Finally, when a provider is renting rather than selling to a large number of customers, that provider faces a disadvantage as the technology involved ages. The provider finds it increasingly difficult to introduce new technology without facing a risk that many of its customers will turn in the rentals they currently have and demand the new technology. Thus, the provider begins to care more about preserving the rental base than about the client's best interests.

Minimize the Client's Risk. As Barbara Bund Jackson, author of *Winning and Keeping Industrial Customers,* noted, "Customers invest in their relationships with vendors in a variety of ways. They invest money; they invest in people, for example, by training employees to run new equipment; they invest in lasting assets, such as the equipment itself; and they invest in changing basic business procedures like inventory handling."[7]

Obviously, the greater the investment, the more reluctant a client will be to change. Although it is impossible to eliminate a client's risk in a service, that risk can certainly be minimized, especially in the early stages of a relationship. Then, as the relationship builds, the opposite strategy can be employed—increasing the investment to gain greater commitment from the client and to buffer yourself against new entrants. There are many ways of doing that with a minimum expenditure for the client. Some useful techniques are:

- Providing a hands-on demonstration or a 30-day trial. (The 30-day guarantee and money-back guarantee have been very important to direct mail successes.) Having used the product will increase a client's comfort with it.
- Making the sale modular. Big pieces are easier to swallow in small bites.

- Making sure, at the outset, that the new product or service is compatible with existing ones, so that clients are not locked into your firm's standard.

- Showing that you sell to prestigious clients. Give new clients success stories and references within their own industry whenever possible. This not only gives them an increased sense of security but also minimizes the buyer's personal risk; the buyer can give examples that show he or she made every attempt to choose a company or service with a proven track record.

- Demonstrating your organization's commitment to the product and/or technology. One way to do this is to have senior management participate in selling and handling the account. Clients will be reassured by knowing that your organization has as much vested in the relationship as they have.

Wait for the Right Opportunity. It is important not to jump at the first opportunity that comes along, but to wait for the right one. The initial entry into the account should not be just a success, but one that the buyer immediately perceives as valuable, so that momentum can be achieved. Be careful to watch for signs that a client is excited about the service. For example, if it has been demonstrated in a similar environment, be careful that your client does not have exaggerated expectations about the service you are providing. Also, be careful that your client's management believes in your service.

Putting It All Together

In the mid-1970s, Xerox, one of the most admired, even legendary, names in America, fell victim to Japanese marketing strategy. Ricoh, a well-known manufacturer in Japan but for all intents and purposes known only for cameras in the United States, developed a plan to market its copiers in the United States. It did not try to market copiers under its own name; it was aware of the prohibitive costs of setting up its own distribution network, the problems involved in developing an image, and its lack of understanding of the U.S. market. Instead, Ricoh selected a company, Savin, that was well-known for selling low-end, inexpensive coated-paper copiers. Savin did not hold a significant market share of the copier business.

Xerox, the market leader at the time, focused on products with high prices and large profit margins. Savin was content with its simple, no-frills product. Because of its image, Savin was not regarded as a threat by Xerox, which marketed its products through company-owned branches. Savin had a distribution network of 400 dealers in all sorts of areas where it was not feasible for Xerox to open branches. Savin quickly became part of the business community, touting its ability to respond quickly to service requests because of its proximity.

Xerox had become complacent. Because of its solid position in the marketplace, it did not maintain an intelligence network to watch for competition. It was so certain of its position that it used a rental strategy, allowing its customers to cancel their rental agreements on one month's notice because it believed they were totally dependent on the product.

When Savin came on the scene, with an aggressive pricing policy that allowed customers to purchase their copiers, Xerox was unable to respond quickly. Soon customers began to cancel their Xerox contracts, replacing the machines with the less expensive Savins. Xerox realized that if it tried to develop and market a similar product, it would soon have warehouses filled with the older, expensive machines returned by its rental clients.

Savin, which had appeared on the scene dramatically, was soon being heralded as one of the fastest-growing companies in the United States. The press referred to its conflict with Xerox as a David and Goliath story. *Fortune* magazine ran a cover story on Savin in March 1978 entitled "Xerox's Fuzzy Future." Simultaneously, *Business Week* placed Savin ahead of 1,200 companies on return on equity. Sales growth was phenomenal—from around $50 million in 1972 to $600 million in 1979. Savin's ads boasted that it was selling more copiers than Xerox and IBM combined.

Throughout this period, Ricoh was devoting a great deal of attention to understanding its customers' mind-set and how dealer operations were run. It was also building a reputation for its products in preparation for one day establishing its own distribution operation.

The story is not yet over. Ricoh has developed an organization in the United States while maintaining its role as the original equipment manufacturer for Savin and Pitney Bowes. (Savin lost much of the momentum it had built up when, in 1982, it decided to manufacture its own copiers, an effort later abandoned. This effort ignored the company's principal strength—marketing and distribution.) Xerox began to fight back. It improved the quality of its equipment, reduced its time to market, strengthened its distribution network, and gained back some of the market share it had lost.

Maintaining an Ongoing Relationship

Among the most important things to remember about maintaining a long-term relationship are the Four Cs: coordination, consistency, continuity, and communication.

Coordination

Clients buy more than services or products; they buy a distribution system, pricing, manufacturing, research and development, service policies, administrative support, data processing, and so forth. Any and all of these elements can play a decisive role in a relationship. The point is to coordinate the efforts of all the functional areas of your organization to serve your clients well.

The best way to do this is to appoint someone in your organization as the primary contact for a client, with the mandate to serve as a clearinghouse for all the relevant information pertaining to that client. All other employees in your organization should receive updated information about the client as soon as it is available, and they should take personal responsibility for doing whatever the account requires efficiently and accurately. As the relationship progresses, your organization must ensure that it has an information system in place to monitor and respond to changes in the account, in the competition, and in your own organization. Your strategic plans should be updated to reflect any changes found. For example, if your competition opens a branch office near one of your client's divisions, your competitor should not have time to make inroads into that division. A representative of your organization should be assigned to make more frequent visits to that division, and special efforts should be made on all levels to assure that your lack of proximity will not be perceived as a negative.

Consistency and Continuity

Sellers should be able to deliver and service products consistently in all buyer locations. There is a basic difference in philosophy between a one-time sale and building a relationship: If errors are made in a one-time sale, a new account can always be pursued. In a lasting relationship, sellers cannot afford to make mistakes. The relationship lives with successes and dies with failures because bad news travels more quickly than good. A Technical Assistance Research Programs study found that the average person who has been burned by a firm tells nine to ten colleagues about that experience, and 13 percent of dissatisfied customers spread the bad news to 20 people. If, for example, a problem develops with service quality at one office location, the minute it is discovered, every effort to minimize the damage must be made. The person in charge of the account should call to explain that the organization is aware of the difficulty and that every effort will be made to correct it. Offers to make amends should be extended. A new machine can be loaned to the customer while the one causing the problem is completely overhauled. Recently, Harris/3M Company "introduced the 'Harris/3M Promise,' a unique three-point product and service guarantee. The company guarantees 98% uptime [on its copiers] or it will refund money for the time the copier is down. It will also provide a free loaner if the copier is out of service for more than eight hours and offers an after-hours toll-free help line to assist customers with minor emergencies."[8] Or, as was the case with a customer of a computerized typesetting equipment manufacturer, when the service department failed to have proper parts in hand for repairs, arrangements were made for the client to use demonstration equipment at the seller's home office that night. The buyer's anger quickly faded when everything was done to ensure that he'd meet his deadline, including providing the salesman's assistance throughout the night.

Theodore Levitt wrote in *The Marketing Imagination* that "the idea is to build bonds that last, no matter who comes and goes."[9] Nevertheless, it is best to keep turnover to a minimum. Turnover hampers continuity, whether it results from promotions, transfers, or attrition. In fact, IBM, once a prime mover of personnel, has changed its philosophy. The *Wall Street Journal* quotes John Akers, its chairman and chief executive officer, as saying, "We've laughed over the years about how IBM means 'I've been moved' and how an executive thinks that every two years, he has to get a new job. . . . Well, that's not possible in today's environment. We need to increase the continuity in the relationship with the customer."[10] When turnover does occur, the damage can be minimized by smooth transitions and good communication. It helps, for example, to see that more than one individual is intimately familiar with the objectives of an account, and it helps to have information systems that provide up-to-date records of that account. It is also useful, for example, in the case of a promotion, to have the original contact keep in touch, if only occasionally, until a satisfactory transition is made.

Communication

This is probably the most important element of all in maintaining a long-term relationship. Information has to be managed. First, set priorities and coordinate what kinds of information and how much of it should be communicated to the account. Be careful that clients are not confused or made apprehensive because they are bombarded with mixed messages. When communications to clients do not come from a central source, conflicting and overlapping messages may be sent. The tug of war that results—Read This First/Buy This First—does not enhance the seller's image.

Be sure your firm presents a consistent image, no matter how many people in how many divisions are involved. This is often a problem when many forms of communication (one-on-one contact, literature, advertising, direct mail, trade shows) are not in sync. When new services and products are rapidly developed, make sure that everyone in the company is aware of them. Communication between clients and salespeople must be open at all times. That is the only way you can keep abreast of a client's needs and respond to them. This kind of communication is facilitated by having those who work directly with a client meet on a regular basis to exchange ideas and discuss the client's current situation.

One excellent vehicle for communication is the account review. Inviting top management in both firms to participate in a performance review raises the level of communication enormously. In 1986, John Anderluh, president of Moore Business Forms and Systems Division, described a performance review as an exchange of perspectives. Sellers report from their point of view, mentioning their understanding of buyers' objectives and recording accomplishments as well as problems; then buyers do the same. Buyers and sellers also explain their objectives for the future.

Anderluh cites impressive results for his company's reviews: "I cannot emphasize enough the high value we place on these meetings. . . . Whenever they have been a part of our national account program, we have yet to lose even one customer due to failure in performance. We have trouble only in those accounts where we have neglected to keep communication lines open."[11]

Conclusion

Relationship management, then, is a uniquely effective way of marketing products or services. As Benson Shapiro explained in *Harvard Business Review,* marketing vehicles are usually measured in terms of their cost and their impact. He explains that advertising is relatively inexpensive as a marketing vehicle in terms of cost per person reached, but its impact is relatively low because a message is standardized and will not appeal to everyone. Moreover, the flow of communication is totally one-way, making response to negative reactions impossible. By contrast, personal selling is expensive, especially on a continuous basis, but its impact is high because two-way communication with a client allows for individualized messages and instant responses to negative impressions.[12]

Relationship management offers the best possible scenario. It is cost-effective because time is spent only on those accounts that have the greatest potential for success. Yet its impact is high because there is ongoing dialogue with the client on current as well as future needs.

The analogy with courtship and marriage is hard to resist. An account should be managed with the same vigor and intensity once the marriage has taken place as it was during courtship. The virtues of relationship management have been extolled by many successful companies. It is a watchword at IBM. As that company's former marketing vice president Buck Rodgers has written, "As far as I am concerned, customer maintenance is imperative to doing business—and can be the difference between a company that struggles to stand still and one that enjoys healthy growth."[13]

8

Managing the Complex Sale

Whether you are selling a service or a product—an operational review, a major computer system, a factory modernization program, a new strategic direction, or a market analysis—a complex sale, one with major implications for both buyer and seller, fully lives up to its name. So many issues arise and so many personalities become involved that it is easy to stumble and fall. Yet, with proper management, a complex sale can provide both buyer and seller great satisfaction and can mark the beginning of a long-term relationship that can be profitable to both.

Understanding the Complex Sale

Before you can deal with a complex sale, you have to understand what it is you are getting into. On the most basic level, a complex sale has major ramifications for both buyer and seller. As a result, complex sales require more patience, more follow-up, and have longer cycles from start to finish than simple sales. Complex sales require greater investments of time, usually involve greater investments of money, and, as a result, usually create greater stress.

Although competition for a complex sale is often great at the beginning, it usually diminishes as competitors decide that they are not prepared to make the commitment required to complete the sale. Communications between buyers and sellers become critical because of the complexity of the relationship both personally and politically. But the effort pays dividends if you manage to become ensconced in a company's inner workings. After relationships are built and territory is established, it becomes much easier to cross-sell other services in the future. The following checklist highlights most of the major characteristics of the complex sale as well as a number of problem areas:

- Significant cost
- Intangible benefits (for example, effect of a new logo)
- High impact (visibility or strategic implications for the buyer)
- Long-term (as opposed to immediate) benefits
- Multiple locations affected
- Low priority given by buyer
- Significant training or reshuffling of personnel required
- Decision postponement will have little immediate impact on the buying organization
- Many functional managers or decision levels involved
- Results not easily measured
- High personal or corporate risk
- New product displaces a previous major investment
- Technology difficult to understand
- Multiple budget centers
- Tremendous changes involved

It is critical for you to keep in mind that certain of these characteristics or barriers are present in every complex sale—even if they do not present themselves immediately. Remember also that many of the psychological barriers that affect a client may *never* come to the surface. Nevertheless, these psychological barriers can still damage relationships, lengthen sales cycles, or cause major objections to be raised later on if they are not ferreted out in the early stages of the sale.

For example, your clients will not always tell you that they have trouble understanding the technology of a product or service or that they don't know how to measure or justify the benefits from a product or service, even though they know intuitively that they should be significant. You will probably never hear some of the war stories about the political problems of getting a similar, previous project off the ground (whose head rolled, for example). Yet even one nagging problem in a client's mind can change the client's reaction to your entire presentation. Only your own understanding of likely problems, even those that will always remain unstated, can minimize the negative impact on the client.

Identify important issues and problems using the checklist; then minimize the objections and stress the benefits of going ahead.

Know All the Players

To accomplish your final goal—making the sale—you have to have a feeling for the role and importance of each of the players in the sale.

Thomas Bonoma explains in an article in the *Harvard Business Review* that the players involved in a sale can be divided into five categories.[1] First, there is the *initiator,* the individual who recognized the problem in the first place and suggested that something or someone out there might be able to solve the problem (whether it is buying a computer or developing a growth strategy). Next comes the *gatekeeper,* the in-house expert who often controls information (and thus your access to corporate decision makers). Third is the *influencer,* the person who has a say in whether or not a purchase is made and which service it is that is ultimately bought. Fourth are the *purchaser* and *user,* who are concerned with obtaining and consuming the best service. Last comes the *decision maker,* whose word is law and who has the last say. Knowing the position of each player in this hierarchy is important in establishing your own relationship with each of them and in helping you decide how to proceed.

What happens if you are dealing with only one person? Actually, the chances are good that you are not, even if that is how it appears on the surface. Usually gray eminences behind the scenes influence your contact and are part of the final decision-making process.

It is essential that you make every effort to find out who these behind-the-scenes individuals are and draw them into negotiations in some way—perhaps by sending along enough information tailored to their needs that they become behind-the-scenes proponents. Doing this is a matter of carefully disseminating information.

I do not mean to imply that you should go over or around your primary contact to try to deal with someone of greater authority. Rather, your goal should be to increase awareness of the benefits of your product or service so that, when the sale is discussed, your case will be seen in the best possible light. For example, you might send out copies of articles that discuss the increased productivity that could be achieved through the use of the computer software you are selling. Copies might be sent to those above and below your contact in the company's hierarchy (and even to other people who, you may suspect, also have a say in the final decision). The worst that can happen is that you will influence someone who has no role in the decision-making process. On the other hand, you have much to gain, because you may succeed in making an important behind-the-scenes ally.

Once you have identified everyone involved in the firm's decision-making process, assess the following four areas of concern.

- *The interests of your client.* It is critical that you learn as much as possible about the personal interests of each individual who will influence the decision to purchase your service. For example, which of the executives you have met has the most to gain from the decision, and which has the most to lose? Does anyone feel threatened by the purchase? Be sure you know enough about each person involved to decide who is most likely to support you and to become the service champion. Direct your approach to that individual.

- *The needs of individuals in terms of their own business units or functional areas.* Will the purchase eliminate something from the budget only over someone's dead body? For example, did that person make the decision on the purchase of the product or service that yours will replace? Similarly, does the product or service you provide require support from an individual or a group that will enjoy no benefit from it? For example, in a number of small businesses, the first group to be computerized is usually the accounting division. When other groups, such as public relations, decide they need computers, the responsibility for choosing the equipment and seeing to its maintenance remains with the accounting division. Also, who will get credit if the project succeeds (or blame if it does not)?

- *The effect that varying perceptions of what you are selling can have at different functional or hierarchical levels.* For example, are you addressing day-to-day problems when explaining the sale to line people and addressing long-term strategy when explaining it to upper management? Are you using enough numbers to satisfy the vice president of finance but too many for the director of communications? For a company that communicates by memo, are you making your points orally in personal meetings? If negative feedback is not part of the corporate culture, can you ask enough of the right questions to make sure that any problems surface?

- *The relationship between members in the decision-making process.* How do you meet one person's needs (or even seem like you are doing so) without slighting the needs or expectations of someone else? Because the selling cycle for a complex sale is so long, how do you keep the client's excitement up and all the players focused? Is there bad blood between some of the players involved? Have certain players cut themselves off from others? If so, how do you get them to attend the same meeting or at least to communicate with one another? Don't make the mistake of thinking that one person's hot button is also another's. As you go from one person to another, you'll see how different each individual's priorities and needs are.

Admittedly, it is extremely difficult to sell to a large group of people. First, people have different needs, which may push you to try to make your service generic so that it will appeal to more constituents. This is as certain to lead to failure as is trying to appeal to the specific needs of a few members of your audience. I once listened to a presentation given by a well-known market research organization to 12 high-ranking members of a corporation. The firm's executives were told that they could acquire economic, industry, and demographic information that would assist them in their strategic planning efforts and would help them identify companies in each branch area that would most need those services. The corporation leaders attending were, collectively, responsible for strategic planning, marketing, research, management of a division, managing a local office, and so forth. Excited by the presentation, each asked questions related to the specific area for which he or she was responsible. After a while, interest visibly faded. No one had had specific questions answered fully, and no one could see the service in terms of the whole organization. The failure to organize the presentation so that everyone thought that their needs had been addressed meant that an opportunity was lost; the corporation did not buy the service.

Dealing with a group presents specific problems that can lead to failure. A major problem is the crowd mentality—everyone waits for everyone else to react. For example, if you feel ill in a crowd and cry out for help, most people will pause for a second, look around, assume someone else will help, and move on. If you instead look someone in the eye and ask for help, "Sir, could you help me to that chair?" the individual addressed is likely to stop and help. A number of others will stop to watch; each of them would then probably also help. In the same way, the market research firm that failed in its presentation could have adopted any of a number of techniques to work against the crowd mentality.

If in a situation such as the presentation mentioned, an agenda that explained the areas to be covered in the presentation had been given out, it could have worked against the crowd mentality. Different specialists could have addressed the specific needs of each corporate leader attending. Even though some executives might have drifted off at various points, they would know their turn was coming. Another solution would have been to break the group into smaller components after a general presentation; then someone could work with the narrower needs of each group. Yet another possibility would have been to identify someone who had some familiarity with your service from an initial meeting and ask that person to mention a few things that interested him or her. (You should use this as an opportunity to choose someone who has the potential to become an advocate of your service.) Getting someone to mention benefits would make everyone else more patient and willing to wait to find out what was in it for them.

Know How to Minimize Risk

The only way to handle the problem of risks is to find which particular risks serve as barriers and then to minimize them. Remember that very few buyers are conscious of their decision-making processes. Think of risk in terms of helping buyers get from "I need it" to "This is the one I want."

Five Types of Risk

The resistance to a purchase that builds during the process leading to a commitment is usually the result of the risk associated with the acquisition. The amount of risk is directly related to the type of buyer and the characteristics of the service. You must analyze the kind of risk the buyer associates with the purchase in order to counter it.

• *Performance Risk.* Will the service do what was claimed for it? What will happen if it does not? For example, think about how you feel when a messenger does not show up with an important document; when a speaker you chose for your organization's national conference bores everyone to tears; when it takes forever to get the bugs out of a phone system you have selected for your company.

No one likes to be associated with a failure. But the amount of risk involved when a service fails to live up to performance expectations varies. The risk increases

- when the decision to purchase has strategic consequences;
- when the failure is particularly hard to remedy;
- when the firm's policies or standards have to be changed in order to implement the decision to purchase;
- when a failure will mean it will be very difficult to catch the competition;

- when a similar decision has never been made before (because the service is untested);
- when, if the service fails to work, opportunities are lost forever.

• *Monetary Risk.* Will I get value for my money? Could I get a better deal somewhere else? In this case risk increases as buyers' costs increase relative to the amount of money they have and to the amount that has to be paid before the service is performed.

• *Status/Position Risk.* Will I damage my reputation with my peers if the service does not live up to the promises I supported? Will the decision win me praise or rejection? What will the decision mean to my status within the organization? In this case the risk depends on

- the individual's longevity and security in an organization (the longer you are with the firm and the better your track record the lower your risk);
- the support the decision gets from top management (the more support, the less likely you are to take the entire blame for failure; moreover the greater their support the more likely it is that the new service can be successfully implemented in the firm);
- the visibility of the decision (if it is a real loser, how long will it take for it to go away?);
- the closeness of the decision to promotion or salary review (or whether the person making the decision has, for example, a new boss).

• *Control Risk.* How much impact does the buyer have over the success or failure of the outcome? Here, the risk increases if buyers have to take someone else's word for the value of the service because they do not have the knowledge to make the decision themselves; if buyers do not understand the service and someone else will have to implement and maintain it; or if success will depend on the service's implementation by others in the organization who are not part of buyers' immediate circles.

• *Unknown Risk.* The unknown that buyers must deal with includes open-ended costs, intangibles, advisers who do not make themselves clear, lack of precedents, and lack of information about variables, such as downside risks.

The Seller's Role

As the seller, you must determine which risks are most likely to affect your buyers' decisions and then try to minimize them. Consider how real these risks may be for buyers before you try to convince them that everything is going to be all right. Remember that the only thing worse than having to confront a risk is having been told that there was no risk when there was one. Always tell the truth: You may have to work a little harder to justify your position, but in the long run you will be ahead—you will have your client's trust.

Many times, risks exist only in a buyer's head. Unfortunately, though, perceptions are often taken for reality. To counteract this, you must project a positive, confident attitude about the sale. You must demonstrate, for example, that the strategy you are selling is the *only* one that a buyer should follow. Emphasize the reputation of your firm and your previous experiences. If you keep in mind the old saying that "no one ever got fired for recommending IBM," you will collect recommendations, endorsements, and evaluations by consumer testing groups that give you that kind of edge. That is why, for example, Bayer claims that doctors would choose its aspirin if they had one medicine to take with them on a desert island and car manufacturers gain sales by advertising that *"Road and Track* magazine rated our product number one for mileage."

In addition, emphasize the *safety* of the purchase; prove to buyers that they are not sticking their necks out by supporting it. You must convince buyers that your service is the best one and that a decision to purchase it will enhance their position. And, naturally, you are the only one who can provide that service.

How can you do this? Perhaps the most important element in reducing risk is education. Your clients should not only be comfortable with you, they should also understand why they are comfortable with you. Make clients understand precisely what you are doing so that they feel in control and can monitor your progress.

You can accomplish this in a number of ways:

- Describe cases that emphasize the successful use of your product or service.
- Provide testimonials to substantiate the benefits of your service either from happy clients or from experts. Crest has used the American Dental Association's Seal of Approval to gain its position as the number one brand of toothpaste.
- Present detailed methodologies and work plans. This is important in projecting the benefits of intangible services; it makes clients believe that they can "almost feel" what you are selling.
- Explain pitfalls or possible problems, because no client ever wants unpleasant surprises. (Even positive surprises can be difficult for some people to deal with, because any unexpected development makes people feel they have lost control.) This not only shows that you know what you are selling but also that you are concerned with its effect on buyers.
- Present fixed costs if possible; clients will be more comfortable and sense less risk if you do so.
- Show that you understand a client's organization and industry and that you can anticipate problems before they ever take place.
- Try to rally support for the decision so that more than one person will champion the cause.
- Present contingency plans so that clients understand that you have thought through the downside of the situation.
- Prove that you have confidence in the service. For example, offer to install computer software for a trial period to allay fears about its quality, or offer a 90-day warranty for it.
- Provide continuity of responsibility whenever possible. If a feasibility study has been sold on the basis of a particular consultant's rapport with clients, that consultant should re-

main visible and accessible throughout the life of the project. This allows clients to feel comfortable with the person responsible for the project's success.

Know How to Communicate Tangible Benefits

The key word here is *benefits:* Give clients what they need, not necessarily what you want them to have. Of course, what clients are really buying is you—and the promise of things to come. After all, when buyers have no way of tasting, feeling, or watching a product or service in operation before purchasing it, they must make judgments largely on the basis of your claims and assertions.

Trust in you and the promise of the satisfaction to come mean that you had better deliver—and also manage your relationship with clients. A great part of this is showing that you understand the problems that are most real to clients—those that they face on a regular basis and are most anxious to solve. Clients often are not interested in any particular features of your product or service except in terms of what the features can do for them.

You will usually not be given the answers to each person's particular needs on a platter. Often you have to probe to discover them at all. Therefore, ask questions, read annual reports, and review speeches by a company's top executives. In short, do whatever it takes to give you the insight you need into the workings of management.

Also, you must differentiate yourself from your competition. When your product or service is perceived to be (justifiably or not) pretty much the same as those your competitors offer, differentiating what you are selling becomes critical.

For example, by determining what the most important issues are to buyers, you can do a better job of illustrating the benefits of your service and how it is superior to your competitors' services. A good case is Tylenol. It seems clear that people buy the company, Johnson & Johnson, as much as or more than they buy the product itself. Tylenol may vary in shape or size from other products in its class, but there is not really much difference in the active ingredients in those products. Tylenol's strong comeback after two major tampering incidents demonstrates that consumers buy Tylenol not just as another pain reliever but as the product of a company that stands behind it and cares about the people who use it.

If you think that selling a service with tangible benefits is difficult, think about the anxiety that selling a service with intangible benefits can cause. For example, when selling computers there are some tangible advantages to demonstrate. It is more difficult, however, to demonstrate the direct benefits of public relations services. All you can do is show that good public relations have helped others, not that yours will do the same. Your past successes can easily be countered by examples of the past failures of other public relations experts who have worked for your potential client.

You can talk for days about the advantages of, say, a unified identity for an international corporation or about how stories successfully placed in the media increased sales. But you cannot prove that either actually makes a difference to a company's future. Your only option therefore is to make some benefits tangible by, for example, conducting pilot testing or market research that allows clients to measure the intangible benefits you have helped bring about.

Know How to Manage the Level of Commitment

As you move along the road to the sale, how can you keep track of where it stands? Is it moving at the rate you think it should or that you want it to? Can you help move it along? The answer is a resounding yes. Before you can step up the pace, however, you have to understand and use the relationships among the sales process, the communications process, and the psychology of the client.

Formula Selling

One of the most commonly used sales approaches is known as formula selling, which is based on steps that correlate with the mental states of prospective clients. Success depends on the ability to

- Attract the prospect's attention;
- Arouse interest through education and by demonstrating your product's capabilities;
- Create a desire for the service by illustrating how its benefits meet an organization's needs; and
- Obtain a client's confidence and support by minimizing risks and building trust.

The selling cycle can be broken into an infinite number of steps that can be monitored on a day-to-day basis for better control of the process. To do this most effectively, various vehicles for communications can be chosen to optimize your efforts, although it is a mistake to think that any one vehicle will always be the best choice (or even the best choice at any given stage in the selling process).

For example, a relationship with a client might start with a totally unsolicited telephone call that must be followed up—perhaps by sending general material about your company and specifics about the service inquired about. Later, you might send newspaper clippings that touch on the problem you're trying to help the client solve (or that simply relate to the client's business and are therefore of possible interest). Also, send the prospective client a copy of your firm's newsletter (if you have one) that is the most closely related to his or her area of interest. Later, make a more specific, yet still informal, follow-up phone call.

Remember to save your ammunition. Do not send out all your marketing material at once. You may save postage, but the message will lose its impact. Even though you are tempted to give them everything you have, buying decisions are rarely made the instant a client opens a marketing package. By sending the material in waves, you keep your company and your service in the client's mind throughout the decision-making process and constantly reinforce your message.

As the selling cycle continues, communications should become more detailed, more client-oriented, and more focused on implementation. For example, advertising and direct mail can be used to create attention. Seminars, surveys, or brochures describing your firm's services can be used to create interest. Finally, case studies of your client's industry and inquiries about specific needs can also create interest.

Barriers to Communications

Little or nothing can be done about some barriers to communications. A memory lapse, a change in priorities, a new competitive position, a corporate bureaucracy, personnel transfers, attrition, new service announcements from competitors, procrastination, and budget cutbacks can all be detrimental to sales. But you may be able to maneuver your way around some of them if you at least know that they exist.

Of course, you cannot prevent a dozen other similar direct mail pieces from arriving at your client's office at the same time yours does or your advertisement from appearing in the same issue of a magazine five of your competitors have advertised in. One way to avoid this kind of problem is not to buy space just because a magazine is giving special rates that month.

Make sure your direct mail is relevant and visually appealing (see Chapter 5 for more detailed information on direct mail). Make sure that it will not arrive the first day after a holiday weekend, when mail piles up on everyone's desk and thus gets less attention, or at a time when prospective clients have their own crunch to worry about (for example, when a company is undergoing a major restructuring). In short, you must be certain that the impression you give is that of someone with the client's business and interests in mind.

Hooking the Client

Your goal is to make prospective clients active, rather than passive, players in the sales process. The communications approach you use should nudge clients along, even if they are unaware of what is happening. By monitoring how close clients are to acceding to your sales approach (closer than a month ago? than two weeks ago?), you can better gauge the probable success of the approach and whether or not you should modify it before proceeding.

Commitment by prospective clients is measured in terms of time, money, and personal risks. As you get closer to a sale, you can tell if commitment increases. The goal of an initial contact is not necessarily to get a sale but to increase a buyer's commitment. People like consistency and stability in their lives, so when they have formed an opinion or made a decision, they do not like to deviate from it. That is why good car salespeople try to get small, even $100, deposits from people planning to purchase $20,000 cars. Once buyers have made this small commitment, they are closer to making purchases. The dialogue usually goes something like this:

> *Salesperson:* I want to make sure that we will have the model you want, if you decide to buy. You see, the car that you're looking at just happens to be our most popular model—after all, most people in this suburb drive their children around a lot, so this car's special safety features make it very popular. In fact, last month we got only two of them, and they never even got to the showroom. For a small deposit—oh, say $100—I can reserve the next one for you.

> *Customer:* What if I change my mind?

> *Salesperson:* No problem. Just call in to cancel. I won't deposit the check. You can either come in and pick it up if you change your mind, or I can tear it up.

Buyers think for a minute and figure they have nothing to lose. The advantage to sellers is that buyers usually cannot resist mentioning what they've done. They tell family and friends that they just put a deposit on a wonderful car, one with the added safety features, even though it is more expensive than other popular models they've been thinking about. That small deposit leads buyers mentally and psychologically to commit themselves to the purchase. The more they talk about the purchase, the more they are committed to it. They are also less likely to think about other possibilities.

This scenario reveals three important points about selling. First, when people express their opinions to family, friends, and colleagues they are much less likely to change their minds. That is why anyone sponsoring a bill in Congress tries to get colleagues to endorse it; then, no matter what the public reaction, colleagues have stated opinions and find it hard to backtrack.

Second, in the beginning of a sales discussion, connect the purchase to values buyers directly endorse. Once buyers can be brought to nod in agreement and thus build an initial positive opinion, they must conclude that their instincts were wrong in order to change their minds—something everyone resists. For example, a car's safety features can be used as an added incentive for purchasing it, especially for women who drive children to school each day. Those features can serve as a reason for moving to a higher priced model than originally anticipated. Parents nod in agreement when the value of safety is mentioned, and that nod is a psychological commitment. Another example is the good saleswoman who spots a successful businessman by his well-cut three-piece suit and thus points out the added value of a car that will impress clients. The businessman, agreeing with the added value of making a good impression, takes a step toward commitment.

Third, the value of patience is incalculable. If a salesperson who worked for the $100 deposit had tried to push for a commitment to purchase instead, the buyer might have walked away in order to think things over. By allowing the buyer the time to think things over, with only a retractable commitment, an experienced salesperson knows he or she stands a far better chance of making the sale. He has increased the sense of commitment on the part of the buyer.

Making a Sale Is a Game of Inches

It is critical to be able to tell when your clients think they want to make a purchase. Being able to judge a client's level of commitment will allow you to prod and nurture the relationship carefully but will not put you in the position of trying to finalize deals too soon. Building commitment is very similar to helping someone climb a ladder in the dark when you are holding a flashlight: Your careful guidance helps that person move to the top, rung by rung. Learn how to increase clients' commitment without making it obvious that that is what you are doing.

Say that you ran an advertisement in a newspaper your prospective clients bought. They made no commitment to your service because they did not know your ad was in the paper. You have no way of knowing that they bought the paper and saw your ad. But if they then call a toll-free number listed in your ad in order to receive some literature, the commitment is beginning. If prospective clients instead call a local number listed in the ad, accepting the price of the call, they are showing a higher degree of commitment. If they are willing to make long-distance calls to pursue the matter, their commitment is even more serious. If they write in explaining their exact interest, they have taken an additional step toward commitment. Calling is done on impulse; writing requires a decision to get in touch and a later decision actually to write the letter—and, for most people, time spent drafting and redrafting the letter.

In the same way, a meeting's structure indicates levels of commitment and provides a guide to how ready prospective clients are to buy. For example, even though clients invest time when they agree to meetings, agreeing to meet at your facility means a greater investment—in travel time as well as in meeting time. If clients bring in colleagues, especially to a meeting in your office, the investment is greater because the costs to clients in terms of work hours have risen. In addition, people who contact you verbally endorse you by convincing others in their organizations that it would be useful for them to attend a meeting. (When clients are attorneys, physicians, accountants, or consultants, who usually charge by the hour for their services, the commitment is strongest.)

Finally, when you provide a 30-day trial of your service based on a buyer's prestated requirements, the potential buyer feels obligated to give you the sale if his or her firm's needs are satisfied. This reaction arises from the fact that people feel uncomfortable being given something and not being able to respond in kind. If you say good morning, most people feel obligated to reciprocate. Or, to take another example, at the Los Angeles airport, the actions of those who are handed flowers by the Hare Krishnas reveal how uncomfortable people are at being given something for nothing. People who are given the flower but do not want to give a contribution try to give the flower back. The cult members refuse to accept them back, saying, "They're yours because we love you." Those who are uncomfortable, but still unwilling to contribute, tend to discard the flowers, nullifying the gift. Hare Krishnas understand this so well that they follow people to retrieve the flowers from wastecans. A more poignant example occurred after World War II. Many veterans in wheelchairs tried to support themselves by selling small items such as pencils or shoelaces. When people would drop money into the containers they held, the veterans insisted that the contributors accept the purchase. The veterans' refusal to take something for nothing meant that they were earning money, not begging; but the size of the purchase price was unimportant. A dollar for a pencil was still a sale, not a contribution.

The last point here is determining when a sale is complete. Is it when the proposal is accepted? When the service is sold? When the client is satisfied with the results? When you have recognized and begun to pursue the next sale? The answer is that you should never consider a sale complete. When you have made a complex sale, you have acquired a new client for future sales.

Know How to Manage the Ongoing Relationship

After you have made the sale and the check is in your hands, start planning your next steps. If there is the slightest chance that you will ever want to do business with the same clients again, go back to square one. You have to continue as if a sale never happened. Continue to manage relationships with your clients to make sure that, if you ever want to call them again, they will be ready to listen.

There are many elements to managing a relationship (see Chapters 7 and 11, on relationship management and service quality, respectively, for more detailed information). These include good communication, honesty, and reliability. (There are a number of traps as well, but overstating benefits and underestimating risks are among the worst.) The main element of a good client relationship is personal trust, and that requires that you build and maintain a reputation as someone who always keeps your word. A major supermarket chain, for example, has signs at checkout counters that say, "The sale isn't finished until you've taken your purchase home and used it." What the signs are saying is, "Trust us. We know you'll be happy with what you've bought because we know you won't be back otherwise." You should be able to say essentially the same thing to your clients after making complex sales.

Maintaining Trust

Of course, you must establish a high level of trust in order to make a sale in the first place. If buyers were not certain that you cared about more than just depositing checks for transactions, you never would have convinced them to buy your high-risk, high-priced, intangible service.

Maintaining that trust is just as important as building it in the first place. As Theodore Levitt said in *The Marketing Imagination,* "The seller has made a sale, which he expects directly to yield a profit. The buyer has bought a tool with which to produce things to yield a profit. *For the seller it is the end of the process; for the buyer the beginning.* "[2] Buyers must believe that their own best interests have been taken into account, that the results of the sale are not simply being dumped in their laps, and that the seller was solid, secure, and experienced in performing the task.

What does this mean to you? It means that the market information and articles you were sending buyers before sales should continue. It also means that you should call to see that everything connected with a sale is running smoothly. It can even mean that, if clients mention problems not necessarily connected to your service but that you have expertise in, you offer advice and counsel. Finally, it means that you make yourself available if problems arise during a transaction or even at some time down the road. If you find out about a problem, never let a client find out about it from a third party (or, worse, through a disaster that happens because the client was not notified).

In short, clients should never feel that they have been used as a means to an end or that the sale was the end of your relationship. Nor should you feel that the relationship ends with a sale. Even after delivery is made and satisfaction assured, you should still consider clients as ongoing sources of new business and referrals, possibly for services not yet developed or additional services as their businesses expand. If you don't think of your clients in this light, competitors waiting in the wings will be only too happy to work on the next sale to *your* clients.

9

Presentations That Persuade

Keep in mind just how much you have at stake every time you make a presentation. You usually do not get a second chance to sell your product, service, or idea to a particular audience; to persuade a board of directors to enter into a new venture; to convince your colleagues that your idea is the one that should be accepted; or even to ask your boss for a raise. The quality of your presentation is also important because of its effects on your and your organization's reputation.

A presentation has to be just right the first time. That requires more than just having a good idea or being right; ideas do not sell on merit alone. A presentation requires clear goals and a sound strategy. You must package a presentation and plan how you will present it. You must create the right environment: Time, location, strategy, even details such as dress are important.

Many people believe that the most critical stage of an effective presentation is the delivery. In fact, the most important element is determining the goals you hope to achieve through the presentation before you develop it. If you start without knowing what you want to achieve, you are leaving too much to chance. You should have in mind a goal that is specific and measurable. Knowing that goal will allow you to realize what action or reaction you want from your audience. It will also help you determine what information you must give your audience in order to get that action or reaction.

Your goal becomes the benchmark against which your arguments can be tested as they are developed. Moreover, once you have a clearly defined goal, it is easier to build a strategy aimed at achieving it. The most important elements of that strategy are knowing your audience, preparing the message and the visuals needed to make your points, and delivering the message.

Taking Stock of the Audience

Once the time and place are chosen, it is time for you to evaluate the audience for your presentation. In *Presentations Plus,* David Peoples compares the material in a presentation to the liquid that is to be poured from a pitcher into a bottle (the audience). The bottle, however, has a stopper in it called "What's in it for me?" Before pouring the liquid into the bottle, you must remove the stopper; you do that by providing a selfish motive that arouses the audience's interest so that it pushes the stopper out of the way in order to receive the liquid (or hear the presentation).[1]

Every audience consists of individuals, each of whose perceptions and motives are unique. The same information will strike different people in different ways: Some will be motivated to act, others will be impelled to resist. People measure the content of a presentation against a myriad of factors, among them personal interests, the impact on their specific business units or functional areas, prior experience and knowledge of a topic, personal prejudice, political values, their tolerance of risk, and the immediate pressures of the day.

Your task is to delve below the surface and detect the underlying elements and common denominators. What are your audience's needs and hot buttons? It may not be possible to appeal to every individual in a group; however, you must still think hard about the people you are addressing. Look at your audience from their point of view. They may be interested and supportive, open-minded and interested in the facts, casual and apathetic, or uninterested and hostile.

In approaching a group that is interested in hearing the facts before making a decision, substance is more important than delivery. Nevertheless, intangibles such as appearance, credentials, and beginning on time are vital, because a first impression may be the deciding factor. Facts and figures need to be stressed, along with expert testimony and specific examples (if possible, examples about people whose situations resemble the audience's). Humor, war stories, flashy visuals, or other fillers may give the impression that you have little to say and may turn off your audience.

On the other hand, dramatic devices are especially effective in dealing with a casual or apathetic group. Here is where your delivery is critical. You must set out to court your audience's attention. Once you have their attention, you must make them eager to hear what you have to offer. You can do this by conveying your own enthusiasm—by presenting what you have to say in such a way that you involve them in thinking about it. Early in the presentation, in order to make sure your audience has an interest in hearing what you have to say, you must answer the implicit question "What's in it for me?" Your efforts in the face of this kind of audience will be damaged by darkening the room, reading your speech word for word (which gives the impression your presentation is generic), or speaking either too technically or in too much detail.

The most difficult of all, of course, is speaking to a group that is hostile or uninterested. When you confront such an audience, remain calm, speak evenly and slowly, and stay in control; if you let the audience's attitude affect you, you will end up encouraging their resistance instead of overcoming it. Keep in mind that nothing fans the flames of resentment more than an I-know-better attitude. Give factual information and data that can be proven and documented. Also, have third-party endorsements at your fingertips that will interest the group and perhaps even arouse their competitive spirit, particularly if the third party is a competitor.

When taking stock of your audience, try to answer such questions as:

- *Who are the decision makers and the people who influence decisions?* If you know the answer to that, or if you can gauge it by noting who in the audience people seem to glance at to check reactions, you can make eye contact with that person on occasion.

If you can get that individual to nod at points you make, you might be able to turn the atmosphere around.

- *Does it have any hidden agendas, rivalries, or obstacles?* For example, if you see that the company's comptroller is present and reacting negatively to the mention of costs, emphasize benefits and favorable comparative costs whenever you can.

- *Is this a captive audience or will other presenters be vying for its attention?* If you think yours is but one of a number of presentations a group will hear, be certain to sum up points in easy-to-remember phrases as you go along. Potential clients who have heard your presentation should have some of your main points in mind as they listen to other presentations.

  One presenter, vying to become the advertising agency of record for a major office products company, knew that he was not the most creative contender and he hadn't had time to prepare and develop a creative media plan because the client's deadline was too tight. He started his presentation by saying so. He spelled out some of the things that could go wrong given the lack of information. Then he said that, with that caveat, he was going to present examples of the kinds of things his agency could do. When the next groups gave their presentations, the client asked them how they could so strongly recommend a campaign without having some of the basic questions answered first—those things the first presenter had alerted them to. It became quickly clear that the other groups had not thought about those problems, and the first presenter ended up getting the client.

- *Can you arrange follow-ups or future contacts?* When you know that you will have such opportunities, don't give all the information at once. For example, if you notice some puzzlement at a bit of technical information you present or are asked a question about something specific, answer briefly and promise to send along more detailed information so that you can reinforce your message and keep audience interest at a peak for as long as possible.

  On the other hand, if you know that this is your one opportunity to meet with people from this organization, give them all the information you can. If those attending the presentation will have to sell your service to their superiors, offer to help with that presentation. Tell them that you could arrange to be at it. If that is not acceptable to their organization, arrange to have an open line during the presentation so that you will be instantly available to answer questions those presenting your service cannot answer. Suggest that they say they have that information in the files and will get an answer after the coffee break. They can use those few minutes to ask you for the answer.

- *Are you being too technical for your audience?* Remember that there is a difference between a member of your audience raising a question about a specific point and missing the entire point of the message you are delivering. The *Wall Street Journal* noted that "the chance to pitch an idea or a new business strategy to top executives can make or break a corporate career. But too often managers blow the opportunity. They talk in technicalities and overload speeches with facts and figures to prove their expertise. In the process they forget their audience."[2]

Commanding the Audience's Attention

The saying "Don't judge a book by its cover" came into use because that is what most people do. Persuasion actually begins well before a word is spoken. As presenter, you have about a minute to create that all-important first impression. In those few seconds, you must gain the audience's acceptance, communicate your qualifications, and provide a compelling reason for your audience to pay attention to you.

You can enhance your credibility in a number of ways:

- *Through symbols.* These include the car you drive and the clothing you wear. They communicate the fact that you are successful. Clothing should also reflect the style of your audience. A three-piece suit in a group that favors blazers, or an elegant silk dress instead of a smart suit, can slow communication between you and your audience by setting you apart. Symbols of success include your titles (such as Ph.D.

or president) and your publications. So send along that white
paper that contains your name and tearsheets of articles you
have written.

- *Citing support.* Endorsements are always useful. They can come
  from someone in the company you are selling to or from
  people or groups with no vested interest in a matter. For
  example, a favorable story in a newspaper about your company or a call from a consultant endorsing you or your company substantiates your claims and lends credibility to
  everything you say.

- *Perception of importance.* It is critical that your audience perceive
  you or your subject as important. Stressing what is new in
  what you are offering gives your audience the sense that they
  can be on the cutting edge if they acquire it. A 1965 study
  by Sears and Freedman shows that communications are more
  effective when audiences believe they contain novel ideas—
  even if they do not.[3]

In an article in the *Public Relations Journal,* Robert Cialdini emphasizes the prevalence of shortcuts among today's audiences
and claims that "citizens of modern Western society no longer
have the time, the energy, or even the mental ability to carefully
weigh the pros and cons of most decisions that face them."[4]
Someone who uses a shortcut will generally focus on one reliable
piece of information. If you are always aware of this, you can use
various techniques to sway your audience. For example, arguments that occur in the beginning or at the end of a presentation
will be remembered more than those that occur in the middle. If
an audience is uninterested, make your most important point
first, to draw them into the presentation. If they are positive or
neutral, the major point can be saved for last, once you have made
some inroads and caught their attention.

In addition, remember that once you have caught your audience's attention, you must maintain it. Experience has shown that
the audience is most attentive during the first 30 seconds and the
last minute of a presentation. In between, their attention slack-
ens. Therefore, it is advisable do something to arouse the audience about every seven minutes. Because of increasing attention
toward the end of a presentation, many speakers will use phrases

like "in summary" or "in conclusion" periodically, indicating the end of the presentation is being reached, even if that is not the case. In addition, a few helpful techniques are:

- Asking rhetorical questions to keep the audience alert.
- Citing relevant examples and war stories.
- Using devices such as metaphors, analogies, and rhetorical questions.
- Mentioning participants by name.
- Using objects or models.
- Adding information received from the audience.
- Using humor, personal experience, and quotations.
- Moving around and maintaining eye contact.
- Asking questions that require audience participation, such as raising hands.

Strengthening the Argument

There are numerous ways to enhance your audience's perception of your service. For example, at times it is best to present one side of an argument; at others, presenting both sides is more effective. A one-sided argument works best when your audience is friendly, when only one speaker is scheduled, or when immediate change is required. Presenting two sides is most effective when an audience is opposed to a speaker or message or when it will hear an opposing view from another speaker. In addition, by presenting two sides, you are perceived to be more objective and to have respect for your audience, which adds to your credibility.

Another frequently used selling device that can be applied to presentations is the illusion of scarcity. People want what they cannot have. This principle is applied by claiming, for example, that a product is available only in limited numbers or only for a limited time. The same principle is at work in one-day sales that department stores hold, in lotteries, and in offerings of limited-edition prints or coins. People also often decide what is right or wrong by the crowd mentality—by observing the actions of others. For example, when an audience is asked if it has any questions after a speech, remember how long it takes for that first hand to be raised and how quickly a half-dozen more are raised once that first one is up. You can use this to your advantage in a presentation by obtaining third-party testimonials or, if possible, endorsements from other divisions of the organization.

Similarly, people are more comfortable making decisions when they have a frame of reference to use for comparison. In a top-down selling approach, a more expensive item is introduced first so that, by comparison, a less expensive one appears to be a bargain. (This is also why maintenance agreements or product accessories are presented after a major sale is completed. Their costs look so small compared to the initial large cost.) In negotiations, an initial request may be large enough to ensure that a second request, which is closer to the figure actually wanted, is seen as a concession and receives a favorable response. However, if the first request is perceived to be unreasonable or extreme, the technique can backfire.

Be sure that you take into account the desire of most people to behave consistently. Once people take a stand, they have a vested interest in maintaining that position and will look for reasons that allow them to confirm that opinion. This phenomenon (as discussed in Chapter 8) is even stronger when an opinion is expressed publicly. As Gerard noted in 1964, publicly stated opinions are more resistant to change than privately held ones.[5] A presenter can leverage this investment factor both with sympathetic and with hostile audiences. When sympathetic audiences are asked for a small initial commitment, they will feel some pressure to follow through on their actions. For example, if you ask them to give you business cards if they want more information, when you follow up, they will feel obliged to listen even if they barely remember what sparked their initial interest. They believe that giving you their cards obligates them to listen to you.

On the other hand, when an audience is not favorably disposed to you, it is better not to challenge their opinions head-on. Do not give them a chance to express negative opinions, because they will then feel obligated to stick to those opinions. Instead, try to neutralize or diffuse their comments until they are more favorably disposed. For example, ask them to accept changes in weakly held beliefs, moving later to the more difficult ones. This is consistent with Moine and Herd's repeated yes technique,[6] in which prospects are induced to say yes to initial ideas so that they will be more favorably disposed toward the rest of an argument.

Visuals*

A 1981 study by the Wharton Center for Applied Research shows that "people are more likely to say 'yes' and act on your recommendations when [you use] visuals. . . . You will be perceived as more professional, persuasive, credible, interesting, and better prepared. The probability of the audience reaching consensus is 79 percent vs. 58 percent without visuals."[7] The evidence points overwhelmingly to the conclusion that a picture is worth a thousand words. Visuals make information easier to understand; they promote interest, improve retention, and allow you to clarify or reinforce key points. The McGraw-Hill Laboratory of Advertising Performance claims that when advertisers use illustrations their ability to stimulate readers to take action increases by 26 percent.[8]

Keep in mind that visuals should never divert attention from your verbal message. For example, turn off an overhead projector when no image is on a screen (or when you take one image off and put a new one on a screen), so the audience is not attracted to white light on a wall.

A few dos and don'ts may be helpful here. In *Effective Presentation,* Anthony Jay cites the seven most common errors made when presenters use slides: They are too verbal, too comprehensive, too complex, too crowded, too colorless, held too long, and not explained.[9] In general, the fewer the lines of type it contains, the more effective a slide is. It is a mistake to try to squeeze too many facts onto one slide, especially without highlighting a main point. Also, visuals should be visual; they are stronger if they are not just words.

*See the Appendix to this chapter for examples of how graphics can be used most effectively.

Evaluating Visuals

The following nine criteria can be used to judge the effectiveness of visuals.

Relevance. Do not present information that is not relevant to the point you are making. As Moine and Herd noted in *Modern Persuasion Strategies,* "Like a movie screen, your customers' interests have limited dimensions. When you project too much information, some of it spills over onto the curtains and the chair tops and the walls, and gets lost in the room."[10] Make sure that your slides move along with your presentation and that an old slide is not on the screen when discussing a new subject.

Purposefulness. It is never wise to tell an audience everything about a subject. However, the other extreme, "anemic" slides can also bore your audience if they lack substance. Keep in mind that anything that does not directly help you accomplish your stated purpose does not belong in your presentation.

Accuracy. Typographical errors, misspellings, and factual errors loom larger than life in visuals. One mistake can make your audience suspicious of your entire presentation.

Visibility. David Ogilvy once asked, "Do you think an ad can sell if no one can read it? You can't save souls in an empty church."[11] For example, the size of the screen you work with will have an enormous effect on the visibility of your slides. David Nadziejka of the Institute of Paper Chemistry has developed ways to determine the screen size you need, as well as the size of the projected images in relation to the room. One of the rules he cites is that "the key for the meeting organizer is to ensure that no one in your audience will be seated farther from the screen than 10 times the height of the projected slide image"; that is, if the image on the screen is, say, 3 feet deep, the last row of seats should not be more than 30 feet away. (He presents other, more detailed rules that are also useful.)[12]

A phrase in capital letters is harder to read than one in uppercase and lowercase letters. In *How to Make Type Readable,* Tinker and Paterson ranked lowercase type 13.4 percent faster to read, as well as more legible and pleasant, than other kinds of type. They also showed that mixing typefaces—creating too much contrast by excessive use of italic, roman, and boldface types—slows reading rates by 8 to 11 percent.[13]

Very wide columns are hard to read because moving the eye over a broad expanse requires more effort. On the other hand, columns that are too narrow also slow readers down because their eyes have to scan too rapidly and rapid eye movements are uncomfortable.

Justify left-hand margins instead of centering text, especially when using bullet points; ragged left margins reduce comprehension 10 percent in reading tests. In a paper for the Ogilvy Center for Research and Development, Colin Wheildon concluded "that ragged setting should be avoided if comprehensibility is to be maintained."[14]

Clarity. Visuals must be legible, comprehensible, and simply stated. Every slide should have a headline emphasizing its main message and focusing the audience's thoughts on that subject. You should also avoid using complete sentences, picking instead phrases that convey your key ideas. This allows you to avoid using periods, which tell an audience, subconsciously, to stop reading.

When making complex or technical points, analogies help the audience paint a picture; they also force them to participate by working to make mental connections.

If you present all your information on one slide and leave that complex slide on the screen for ten minutes, you run the risk of boring your audience or having them spend their time trying to figure out the material on the screen instead of listening to you. When you do not want to give information all at once but want to go into detail, use a sequence of slides, each containing a component of your information. Slides can build the picture you are trying to convey. On the other hand, when you use such builds to present an overall concept, you will end up flicking through slides too quickly. Instead, show the overall concept first, then break it into relevant pieces.

Tables should be used for actual numbers, while charts can show trends, comparisons, and relationships. In addition, charts also clarify and condense a great deal of information. Be sure you choose the right type of chart for each function. For example, bar charts are best used for comparisons; pie charts for highlighting relationships among parts of a whole; graphs for changes and trends; and diagrams for clarifying complex structures. (Also, when preparing graphs or charts, lettering must be horizontal to avoid distracting your audience.)

Customization. Customize your presentation. People appreciate being considered special. They assume that if you consider them special enough to make such an effort, you will continue to treat them just as well when they are clients. If cost or timing is an issue, you can customize presentations by inserting extra slides at various points that refer to something specific to the new client you are wooing. For example, your diagram of how your service affects an organization can be redone to match the structure of the particular organization you are making the presentation to. One replacement slide aimed at each specific client can have an enormous effect.

Interest. Color helps keep your presentation interesting, but do not use more than three colors per slide. Dark colors like blue, violet, and green have short wavelengths and are difficult to read against dark backgrounds, because they tend to blend in. It is best to maintain high contrast by using, for example, yellow on black, black on white, or white on blue.

Ease of Recall. Two months after a presentation, people have forgotten 75 percent or more of what they heard. Anything that you can do to keep your material simple will help. For example, round off numbers, and follow up your presentation with other communications that reinforce your message.

Impact. A few hints:

• When making a request, provide a rationale. Instead of just asking for something to be done, explain why it has to be done.

- Explain cost by breaking it into its smallest components, so that it appears to involve less of a commitment than the total cost. For example, $.50 a day sounds a lot better than $183 a year.
- When presenting facts, make sure your sources are as credible as possible. In some cases, citing the *New York Times* carries more weight than citing *People* magazine.
- When using testimonials, remember that an audience will become suspicious if faced with too many.

Some Final Notes

Numerous other elements are important in preparing a presentation. Many of them seem self-evident, but you can lose sight of them as you collect information about your clients and their firms, as you work on visuals, or as you make sure your firm is ready to do the necessary follow-up. For example, once it becomes clear that a formal presentation is the next step in selling your product or service, you should carefully control its place and time. Because your delivery is also critical, be sure that you allow sufficient time to plan and practice your presentation and that you are fully prepared to answer any questions your audience may ask.

Place

If at all possible, do not make presentations in clients' offices. There they are likely to be distracted by phone calls and other interruptions as well as day-to-day business. If presentations have to be made on clients' premises, see if they can arrange for you to give them in conference rooms. Then, try to get appointments to see the rooms before your presentation, and be sure to make arrangements for all the equipment you need—a computer, an easel, or a screen—to be available.

If you are hosting a large event such as a press conference, keep in mind that it is always better to choose a room that is five chairs short than to have a room that is half empty—having to bring in extra chairs makes the event look important. Also make sure that the location is in keeping with your theme. If you are presenting a formal research finding, it would be better to hold it at a university than in a fancy restaurant. If you are holding the meeting in a hotel, be careful that you are not near the kitchen, and check to see that the adjoining room will not be used for something that will create a lot of noise. Also be careful to check on small details: Does the room have an individual thermostat? Is your event listed prominently on a board near the hotel's main entrance? Will there be water and glasses available?

As noted in the last chapter, a presentation at your firm's headquarters gives you the advantage of forcing an initial commitment from your clients; they spend time and money coming to hear what you have to say, which means that they have already made an investment in you. In addition, a presentation on home ground is more comfortable for you. And it means that your clients can think about what you have presented as they return to their offices.

Time

To ensure that you have your audience's undivided attention, remove as many obstacles to concentration as possible. Depending on a client's business, it might make more sense to meet early in the morning, when the day's problems have not yet presented themselves. In other cases—for example, when dealing with a financial services firm that does a good deal of business in Asia—the afternoon might be better. Early morning is when those firms evaluate what happened in the Japanese markets to determine their strategy for the day. Try to avoid doing a presentation before your clients have big meetings, when they will be preoccupied, or late on Friday, when they are tired and focusing on the weekend. Also, avoid doing presentations right after lunch; if your clients have had heavy meals, they might be tired.

One of the most popular times to hold meetings is late morning. In some fields, such as publishing, a lunch following a meeting allows for further interaction. It is a stage for resolving details, answering remaining questions, and even for informally sealing a deal. But no matter what field you are in, following a meeting with a good lunch leaves your client with favorable memories. A

1985 study by Janis, Kaye, and Kirschner found that the extraneous gratification of eating while reading persuasive communications tended to increase their effectiveness.[15]

Delivery

The most persuasive element in your presentation is the enthusiasm you convey. The impact of your presentation will be stronger if you can find ways to evoke active rather than passive participation from your audience. Instead of sticking to a rigid plan, you will be much more effective if you pick up cues from your audience as they respond to the presentation. If they seem more interested in one aspect of a proposal, emphasize everything pertaining to that element as you come to it. A presentation that is memorized or read will be less persuasive because you cannot respond to cues from your audience. As for length, it is better to be too short than too long or to have to rush through the most important points because too much detail was added up front.

Questions

Before making a presentation, anticipate questions that your audience may ask. Good persuaders do not rebut other people's objections to their arguments. They acknowledge and rephrase those statements, then restate their own points, showing their merits. In fact, if you face a hostile audience, you would be wise to avoid a question-and-answer session that might cause you to lose control. It would be more effective to conclude the presentation or have a break in it, isolate those individuals that seem most skeptical, convince them, and then reconvene.

Good persuaders always admit that they do not know the answer to every question. They also discourage people from deviating from the subject by asking for irrelevant information or by trying to dominate discussions.

Follow-up

A 1964 study by Watts and McGuire showed that the effects of persuasive communications tend to wear off in time.[16] This is a good reason for you to use additional vehicles to support and continue your message. Materials you leave behind are also important because they continue to persuade and reinforce when you are not present. In addition, they have the advantage of delivering information that your clients are comfortable with, because your presentation has taught them enough so that they understand most of what they see without any difficulty—it is familiar territory. Such materials are also of value because they can be given to decision makers who did not attend your presentation. A caveat is important here: Generally speaking, materials to be left with an audience should be given out *after* a presentation; do not hand out printed matter before your presentation. The material will distract your audience; people will flip through it during your presentation.

Conclusion

A persuasive presentation requires clear goals, a sound strategy, and careful planning, whether you are asking an individual or a group to adopt or revise an attitude, accept or modify an opinion, take action or refrain from acting, or make a decision. These situations are critical because they result in a win or a loss. Being half as good as your competition will not ensure that you receive half the rewards they do. In business, as in war, there are no consolation prizes.

Appendix

A Picture Can Be Worth a Thousand Words

As we have just discussed, the visuals that accompany your presentations can be critical to your success. Graphics are a means of strengthening your presentations, making material clearer and more appealing to your audience. But remember that graphics are more than entertainment; they help maintain your audience's interest and keep their attention focused on the points you are making. They improve the effectiveness of your presentation by helping the audience remember critical information and by leaving them with images that reinforce the message you are delivering.

On the following pages, you will see examples of correct and incorrect ways of preparing visuals. On the top of each page is a visual representing one typical incorrect way to present information; we have then taken the same information and reformatted it to improve its readability, clarity, and impact. These visuals, developed with and then prepared by Andy Corn, president of ADMASTER, Inc., of New York, will clarify a number of points made in Chapter 9.

OVERVIEW

Our company's sales rely on a long standing stable customer base. This customer base has been established through extensive client planning and superior service delivery. This has enabled us to achieve a reliable cash flow and predictable margins. Our profits have enabled us to make recent equipment upgrades which have led to rising asset values. In conclusion, we are in a unique position to service our present clients.

OVERVIEW

■ Stable Customer Base
■ Reliable Cash Flow
■ Predictable Margins
■ Rising Asset Values
■ Conclusion: Ability to Service

If you want your audience to concentrate on what you are saying, do not give them large blocks of text to read. Lists of key phrases emphasize and reinforce your points.

OVERVIEW

Stable Customer Base

Reliable Cash Flow

Predictable Margins

Rising Asset Values

Conclusion: Ability to Service

OVERVIEW

■ Stable Customer Base

■ Reliable Cash Flow

■ Predictable Margins

■ Rising Asset Values

■ Conclusion: Ability to Service

Do not try to be overly creative in setting up a list. Remember that we are trained to read from left to right. Help the audience find the start of each line by anchoring a list with bullet points.

OVERVIEW

- Stable Customer Base
- Reliable Cash Flow
- Predictable Margins
- Rising Asset Values
- Conclusion: Ability to Service

OVERVIEW

- Stable Customer Base
- Reliable Cash Flow
- Predictable Margins
- Rising Asset Values
- Conclusion: Ability to Service

Do not create artificial borders on a slide. Take advantage of the maximum visual area of a slide.

At 2:45 pm, Wednesday, December Second, There Was a Sudden Impact Between Two Cars on the Corner of 21st and Broad.

Visuals make information easier to understand, promote interest, improve retention, and allow you to clarify or reinforce key points.

Administration

- **Decentralized Day-to-Day Operations**
  - Local Management
  - Customer Service Oriented
  - Satellite Management
- **Decentralized Management Team**
  - Hands-On Key Account Approach
  - Benefit Personnel
  - Local Knowledge
- **Decentralized Billing**
  - Sales
  - Collections
  - Reporting

Administration

- Day-to-Day Operations
- Management Team
- Billing

Don't try to squeeze too many points onto a slide. The slide should highlight key points only.

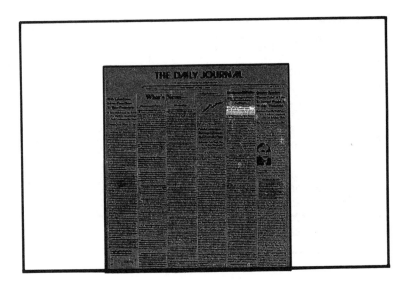

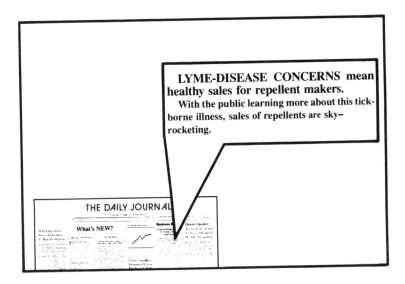

Highlighting adds impact, because the legibility is key. One way to achieve this is to magnify the material you want to emphasize.

Business Start-Ups
- Seed Capital
- Computers
- Legal Fees
- Phones, Fax and Telex
- Accounting Fees
- Sales and Marketing
- Bookkeeping
- Operations and Equipment
- Business Plan
- Advertising
- Marketing Plan
- Personnel

The more lines of type you put on a slide, the smaller the type size and the less readable. Putting the same material on two slides allows you to increase the type size.

Business Start-Ups
- Seed Capital
- Computers
- Legal Fees
- Phones, Fax and Telex
- Accounting Fees
- Sales and Marketing

Business Start-Ups (cont.)
- Bookkeeping
- Operations and Equipment
- Business Plan
- Advertising
- Marketing Plan
- Personnel

OVERVIEW
- **Stable Customer Base**
- Reliable Cash Flow
- Predictable Margins
- Rising Asset Values
- Conclusion: Ability to Service

OVERVIEW
- Stable Customer Base
- **Reliable Cash Flow**
- Predictable Margins
- Rising Asset Values
- Conclusion: Ability to Service

OVERVIEW
- Stable Customer Base
- Reliable Cash Flow
- **Predictable Margins**
- Rising Asset Values
- Conclusion: Ability to Service

OVERVIEW
- Stable Customer Base
- Reliable Cash Flow
- Predictable Margins
- **Rising Asset Values**
- Conclusion: Ability to Service

OVERVIEW
- Stable Customer Base
- Reliable Cash Flow
- Predictable Margins
- Rising Asset Values
- **Conclusion: Ability to Service**

Builds are a very useful way of leading your audience from point to point. Different lines are highlighted as the speech progresses.

OVERVIEW

- Stable Customer Base
- Reliable Cash Flow
- Predictable Margins
- Rising Asset Values
- Conclusion: Ability to Service

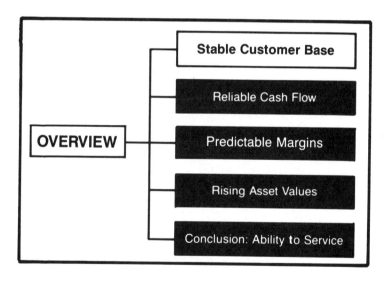

You can present the same material in a number of ways. Try to vary the slides, changing from simple type to graphics at different times to maintain interest.

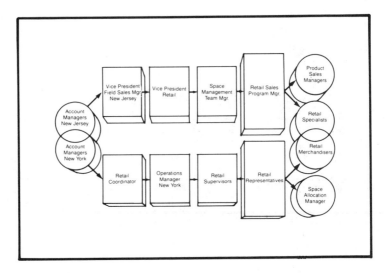

Complicated diagrams can be difficult for an audience to comprehend when presented as a total concept. One solution is to lead the audience through the central points with a build.

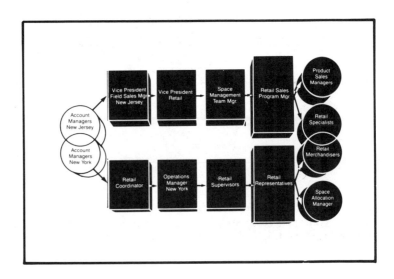

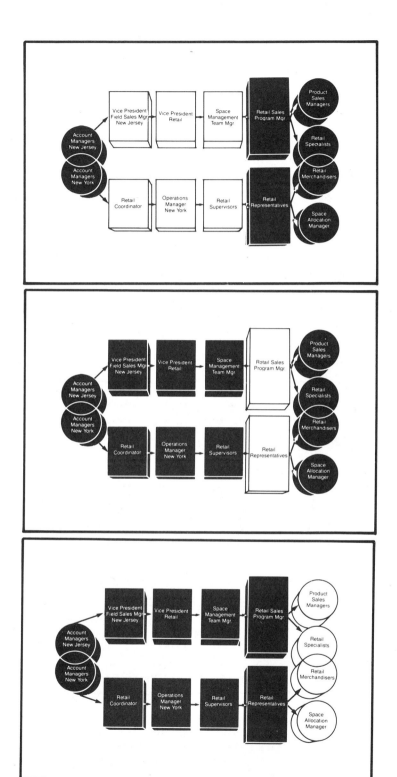

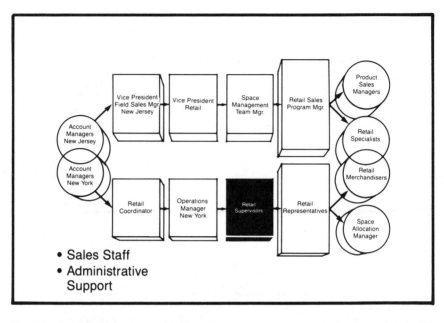

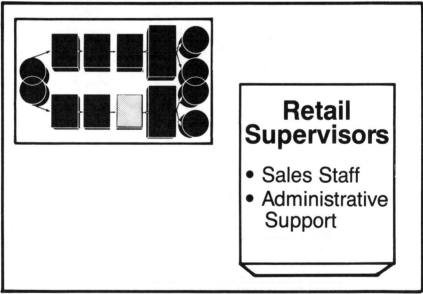

Use color to highlight the section of a complex slide you are
discussing. By retaining the broad picture, you allow the reader to
place the material in a broader context. The central message must
be prominent on the slide. A diagram already presented can take
on a lesser visual role.

The Decade's Leaders in Underwriting

Top Leaders	$ Billions
John	30.8
Paul	16.4
Joan	14.1
Joe	12.6
Bob	9.7
Laurie	8.9

Source: Information Services

Your audience cannot slip a piece of paper under each line to read across. Either move the two columns together, use leaders to connect lines, or give each line an alternating color for better readability.

The Decade's Leaders in Underwriting

Top Leaders	$ Billions
John	30.8
Paul	16.4
Joan	14.1
Joe	12.6
Bob	9.7
Laurie	8.9

Source: Information Services

The Decade's Leaders in Underwriting

Top Leaders	$ Billions
John	30.8
Paul	16.4
Joan	14.1
Joe	12.6
Bob	9.7
Laurie	8.9

Source: Information Services

Forward moving	═══*FORWARD MOVING*
Conservative	**Conservative**
Straight	STRAIGHT
Hot	**Hot**
Heavy	**HEAVY**
Aggressive	**Aggressive**
Push	*Push*
Pull	Pull
Soft	*Soft*
Yell	*Y-E-L-L*
Jump	J^{u}m^p

When properly chosen, typefaces can be used to help convey your message.

OVERVIEW

- STABLE CUSTOMER BASE
- RELIABLE CASH FLOW
- PREDICTABLE MARGINS
- RISING ASSET VALUES
- CONCLUSION: ABILITY TO SERVICE

OVERVIEW

- Stable Customer Base
- Reliable Cash Flow
- Predictable Margins
- Rising Asset Values
- Conclusion: Ability to Service

A phrase in capital letters is harder to read than one set in upper and lower case. Studies rank lower case 13-14% faster to read, as well as more legible and pleasing to the eye.

Administration

Controls

■ *Centralized Management Team*
  - Pricing and Purchasing
  - Centralized Billing
  - Daily Reporting of Sales & Receipts
  - Satellite Management

■ *Decentralized Day-to-Day Operations*
  - Local Management
  - Customer Service Oriented

Administration

Controls

■ Centralized Management Team
  - Pricing and Purchasing
  - Centralized Billing
  - Daily Reporting of Sales & Receipts
  - Satellite Management

■ Decentralized Day-to-Day Operations
  - Local Management
  - Customer Service Oriented

Studies show that mixing typefaces, such as italic, roman, and bold typefac
slows reading rates by 8-11%.

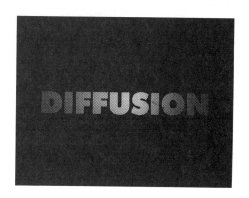

Special effects and attention getting devices make a presentation exciting, and are particularly useful during long presentations.

Domestic Bond Service Centers

New York
- Home Office
- MIS Mainframe
- Agency Presence

New Jersey
- Regional Salesforce
- Increased Market Share
- Distribution Center ·

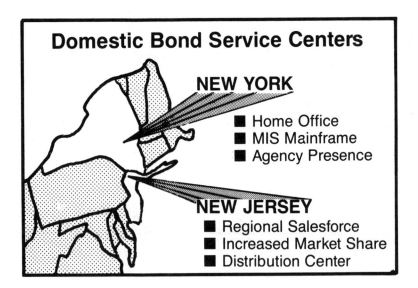

Type can be combined with special effects to highlight key points or maintain interest.

Growth in Sales

Year	$ Millions	Increased Percentage
1970	40.1	-
1975	70.3	+75%
1980	95.2	+35%
1985	160.6	+69%
1990 (Projected)	205.7	+28%

Charts should be used to show trends, comparisons, and relationships. Graphs should be used to illustrate changes and trends. Bar charts are best used when you want to make comparisons.

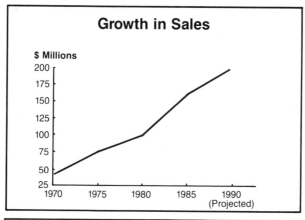

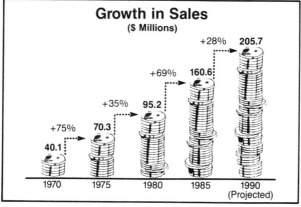

Sales and Net Income Growth

	1986	1987	1988	1989
Sales	110	118	125	165
Net Income	23	25	30	60

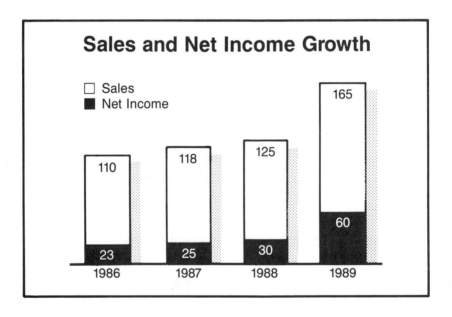

Bar charts are best used when you want to make comparisons.

Administrative Expenses

	Percent
Insurance	30
Legal	10
Printing	10
Supplies	20
Office Equipment	30

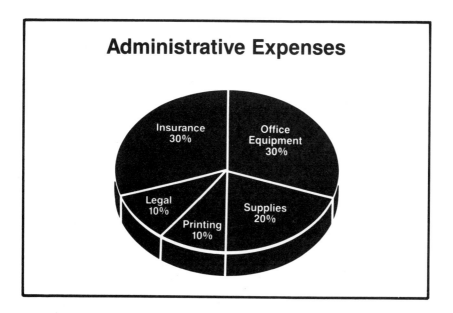

Administrative Expenses

Pie charts are best used when you want to show the relationships between parts of a whole.

10

Barriers to Communication

Seven out of every ten minutes that you and I are conscious, alive, and awake, we are communicating . . . and that communication time is devoted 9 percent to writing, 16 percent to reading, 30 percent to speaking, and 45 percent to listening.

—*Paul Rankin*[1]

Communication takes many forms. We give direction, share opinions, ask and answer questions, provide information, instruct, advise, motivate, persuade, argue, network, council, and gossip. These activities all contribute to identifying new business opportunities, building personal relationships, addressing problems, implementing decisions, and satisfying client needs. When it comes to business, the costs associated with poor communication can be devastating—missed business opportunities; poor customer service; lost time, energy, money, and productivity; and strains in business relationships.

The authors of *Effective Listening* relate a story that so clearly shows the effects of poor communication that it is worth repeating:

A new employee approached one of the women in our office with an important looking paper in his hand, pointed to the paper shredding machine, and asked her to show him how to operate it. "Of course," she said, "you just turn the switch on here, put your sheet of paper in here, like this, and that's all there is to it." As the machine devoured his document, the new man thanked her for her help and then asked, "By the way, how many copies will this make?"[2]

How many times have you had salespeople try to sell you something that they were instructed to try to move, annoying you and perhaps causing you to walk away instead of finding out what your needs were? How many times have you given instructions to employees before you left on a trip only to find that you lost a business opportunity when you got back because your instructions were misunderstood? How many times have you attended a meeting with someone only to discover that you and your colleague had completely different views of what transpired? How many times do you feel like exploding on the telephone, not so much because of the problem that motivated the call but because you cannot get anyone to listen and connect you with the person who could solve the problem?

The need to be heard—and the recognition that all too often we aren't—is something everyone cares about. A report on healthcare in the *Wall Street Journal* shows how pervasive the communication problem is:

> Recent healthcare research shows that what patients want most from a doctor's appointment is, first, a chance to tell their story, and second, information about their problem and how to solve it. . . . Poor communication between doctors and patients is the single most common cause of malpractice suits according to an article last year in the *Maryland Medical Journal.* Doctors who are arrogant or otherwise poor communicators are easy marks for malpractice lawyers.[3]

It Takes Two to Communicate

Even though, as noted in the quotation at the beginning of the chapter, 45 percent of our communication time is devoted to listening, when report cards are given out to business people on how well they listen, very few receive passing grades. In fact, according to a *Harvard Business Review* article, "Immediately after the average person has listened to someone talk, he remembers only about half of what he has heard—no matter how carefully he thought he was listening. . . . Two months after listening to a talk, the average listener will remember only about 25 percent of what was said."[4]

The problem arises because most people have never really learned how to listen properly. Many people believe that communication is the sole responsibility of the speaker, not a process involving both speaker and listener. Furthermore, many business people believe that listening ends when a speaker stops speaking, ignoring the critical processes of understanding what was heard, evaluating the information, and finally determining what action is required.

In business, communication is further complicated because employees who are part of the same organization may have very different specialized languages and many different perceptions of the business—yet they still need to communicate. Dr. Ralph Nichols, sometimes referred to as the Father of Listening, explains the problem as a considerable falloff in understanding as you move down the organizational ladder. He explained that between the top level of management and just one level below, there was a 34 percent loss of understanding in communications. The problem continues as communications move down through the organization. At the level of "plant manager 40 percent arrives. At the foreman level, 30 percent; and in 100 representative American industries only 20 percent of the communication sent downward through five levels of management finally gets to the worker level."[5]

There are many reasons for this failure to communicate: lack of similar context, assuming that others know what is happening (after all, we know, why don't they?), poorly expressed communications, difficulty in dealing with those on a higher level and a resulting failure to question them when they are unclear, inability to read nonverbal signals, and, perhaps most important, an inability to listen properly.

Barriers to Listening

Understanding the needs of new clients or selling new products or services to existing clients requires good communication skills. That means, among other things, knowing how to listen. But as

Nichols noted, most people have poor listening habits.[6] These can, however, be overcome if we are conscious of them and how they affect us.

Assuming a Subject Is Uninteresting. Do you prejudge upcoming meetings, often assuming they will be dry or boring? Do you selectively tune in and out of conversations because it takes people too long to get to the point? Do you think you can use your time more productively than by attending meetings and thus rebel by daydreaming?

Good listeners try to hunt for nuggets of information that they can use or apply later on. They believe that if they have to attend a meeting, they might as well make the best of it. Bad listeners conclude that a meeting isn't worth their attention after a few sentences and decide their time would be better spent on unrelated subjects.

Focusing on Delivery.   Do you place more emphasis on speakers than on what they say? Do you know just by a person's appearance and delivery that he or she won't have anything worthwhile to say? Do you find yourself thinking, "If he cracks that gum one more time . . ." or "I wish she'd stop reading her notes" or "His visuals were amateurish"?

Good listeners focus on content rather than on delivery. They think to themselves, "This guy should clean up his act, but if he didn't know the subject matter, he wouldn't have been invited to speak. I'd better find out what he knows."

Reacting Too Quickly.   Do you evaluate a speaker's message before he or she has finished a single thought? Do you get so excited about something in the middle of a conversation that you want to run out and tell everyone the good news? Do you get so angry when something or someone hits a nerve that you want to climb over the conference table and pounce on the speaker?

Good listeners reserve judgment until they thoroughly understand a message. Bad listeners tune out once they have heard something that triggers an emotional reaction; rather than listening to the rest of the message, they then spend their time planning a rebuttal or preparing a question they hope will embarrass the speaker.

Reacting to Emotional Words. Do certain speakers, issues, words, or points of view set you off whenever you hear them? Do you make a concerted effort to understand other points of view?

Your emotions affect your listening. For example, sometimes prejudices and deep convictions cause you to block out much of what a speaker you don't like is saying. At other times your admiration of a speaker makes you ignore the fact that what is being said is useless or incorrect.

People have blind spots just as cars do. But good listeners know their strong beliefs and emotional biases and do not let them interfere with their listening abilities. You must be aware of the natural tendency to judge, evaluate, and approve or disapprove of the words and opinions of other people.

Listening Primarily for Facts. Do you listen primarily for facts, or do you try to understand and absorb ideas? When listening to a speech, do you try to memorize every fact? Do you get so involved in facts that you miss nonverbal clues?

Every time they recognize a fact, some people stop listening to file it away. They don't realize that while they are trying to memorize the first fact, they are missing the message it was meant to support. Trying to ferret out a speaker's main points is much more important than hearing a lot of facts that don't tie together. You also face the danger of becoming so wrapped up in noting down facts that you fail to note that a speaker is using, say, a facial expression to negate the importance of a fact he or she is stating.

Inflexible Listening. Do you impose your personal speaking style on other speakers? Do you tune out when speakers do not organize their speeches from the general to the specific? Do you find yourself thinking, "Come on. What's the bottom line?"

Less than half the formal speeches given are carefully organized and outlined. Listeners who think they must outline presentations mentally are not paying enough attention to get speakers' messages. Good listeners are much more flexible; they take notes casually, jotting down facts or ideas, points or principles that may prove useful in the future.

Pretending to Listen.   When people talk, do you try to make them think you are listening when you're really not? Have you ever asked a question that was a dead giveaway to the fact that you hadn't heard what the speaker said?

Good listeners maintain eye contact with, ask questions of, and send nonverbal cues to speakers to indicate that they are attentive, interested, and carefully listening. They know that being a good listener requires patience, effort, and concentration. If good listeners don't have the time to listen, they let speakers know beforehand rather than fake attention. Poor listeners think that if they don't understand a message or are bored with the delivery, it is the speaker's fault. So they fake attention and let their minds wander.

Permitting Distractions.   Do you suddenly turn away from the person you are speaking to in order to shout instructions to an employee walking by? Do you allow your secretary to remind you of appointments, give you plane tickets, or ask you to sign letters while you are talking to others? Do you grab your telephone while in a meeting or put someone on hold in the middle of a conversation?

People have a finite capacity for listening; they cannot listen to many conversations at once. Therefore, good listeners limit distractions. They close doors, put down their pens, stop flipping through papers, turn off their telephones, do not wave to passersby. In other words, they give their undivided attention to a conversation.

Avoiding Difficult Subjects.   Do you ask for clarification of a point that you do not understand, or do you try to figure it out as a speaker continues talking? Do you avoid listening whenever a subject is unfamiliar?

Poor listeners are inexperienced in listening to difficult material. As soon as they see a technical chart, a set of numbers, or a complicated diagram, they tune out. Good listeners have an appetite for learning. They try to research subjects beforehand so that they have a base of knowledge that they can build on.

Adjusting Our Minds to the Slow Speed of Speech. According to a *Harvard Business Review* article, "We think much faster than we talk. The average rate of speech for most Americans is about 125 words a minute, [but] words race through our brains at speeds much higher than 125 words per minute. This means that, when we listen, we ask our brain to receive words at an extremely slow pace compared with its capabilities."[7]

Your natural tendency is to think about a golf outing, a family or business problem, or the next meeting in order to fill the spaces between words, assuming that you can track the conversation while doing so. Unfortunately, what happens is that you get absorbed in unrelated thoughts and fail to hear what you may need to hear.

Six Perspectives on a Situation

One powerful technique that can be used to improve your ability to grasp communications and to enhance the way you think about and evaluate new ideas was developed by Dr. Edward de Bono, a leading authority in the field of conceptual thinking.

In his book, *Six Thinking Hats,* de Bono suggests that by role playing, people can overcome many of the automatic responses that often get in the way during a decision-making process. For example, people often use the expression "let me play devil's advocate," meaning that they will switch gears and try to find holes in a recommendation or argument that they really support. Some marketing executives use that technique to help their colleagues prepare for a presentation. They will ask the presenter questions from the client's perspective, helping prepare the presenter for every eventuality.

According to de Bono, the ability to look at things from all sides can be developed by mentally putting on six different hats, each representing a different, instinctive way of looking at something.

De Bono says that the first hat, the white hat, is the one that allows us to be "neutral and objective. The white hat is concerned with objective facts and figures. . . . It is clear that white hat thinking excludes such valuable things as hunch, intuition, judgment based on experience, feeling, impression, and opinion. That is, of course, the purpose of having the white hat: to have a way of asking only for information."[8]

The second hat is a red one, the color of anger. Putting on this hat allows the wearer to take an emotional view. De Bono says that "the most difficult thing about wearing the red thinking hat is resisting the temptation to justify an expressed emotion. Such justification may be true or it may be false. In both cases, red hat thinking makes it unnecessary. . . . Never mind why you mistrust him. You mistrust him."[9]

The third is the black hat—the color signifying gloomy, negative perspectives. With it the wearer sees why something can't be done. According to de Bono, black hat thinking helps us to figure out what is "wrong, incorrect, and in error. It relieves the thinker of the need to be fair and to see both sides of the situation."[10]

The fourth, the yellow hat, reflective of the sun, helps us see positive aspects. "The yellow hat is optimistic and covers hope and positive thinking . . . yellow hat thinking is constructive and generative. From yellow hat thinking comes concrete proposals and suggestions"; it helps us make things happen.[11]

The fifth, the green hat, is the color of growing things. De Bono says that "the green hat indicates creativity and new ideas. . . . The green thinking hat is specifically concerned with new ways of looking at things. Green hat thinking is concerned with escaping from the old ideas in order to find better ones."[12]

The sixth and final hat, the blue hat, is

the color of the sky, which is above everything else. The blue hat is concerned with control and the organization of the thinking process . . . the conductor of an orchestra calls up first the violins and then the wind section. The conductor is in control. The conductor is wearing the blue hat. What the conductor does for the orchestra, the blue hat does for thinking. Wearing the blue thinking hat, we tell ourselves—or others—which of the other five hats to wear. Blue hat thinking tells us when to switch hats. If thinking is to be a formal procedure, then the blue hat is in control of the protocol.[13]

Practicing wearing these hats improves your ability to evaluate what you hear. It helps break down the barriers to good listening, and that enables you really to listen to what your clients say, understand the problems they are facing, and thereby improve all of your business relationships.

There Is More to Communication Than Words

Words are only one element of communication. In fact, "research indicates that facial expression along with tone of voice accounts for more than 90 percent of the communication between two people. The dictionary meaning of words, then, accounts for only about 10 percent of the communications."[14] Research also confirms that "when verbal and nonverbal messages contradict each other, we have a tendency to believe the nonverbal message."[15] For example, if management says that it wants to reduce the class system in an organization but provides executive spaces in the company parking lot and an executive dining room, all its statements about eliminating hierarchies are suspect.

Many misunderstandings and misinterpretations occur because of a tendency to overlook the numerous factors that affect communication. Remember that what you hear is colored by room design, spatial distance, timing in speech patterns, variances among different cultures, body language, tone of voice, and facial expressions. Given how easy it is to tune out, keep all these elements in mind when trying to communicate information to clients and when listening to what they have to say.

Physical Environment

Physical settings can be used to support or enhance messages. This is a lesson every politician has mastered. For example, when President George Bush presented the details of the 1989 Governors' Summit Conference, he did so at the foot of the Jefferson Memorial (Jefferson is considered the education president); when Martin Luther King, Jr., delivered his famous "I have a dream" speech, he did so at the Lincoln Memorial. Because people's attention tends to wander when listening, speakers can try to choose a place that will make an audience think about related subjects, thus reinforcing their messages.

It is just as important for business people to examine the physical environment that supports or contradicts their verbal messages. To avoid constructing barriers to communication, you may want to hold meetings in conference rooms rather than in offices, because a person sitting behind a desk is in a superior position. Also, control the signals the table in the room gives. With a round table, no one sits at the head of the table so everyone feels equal—and free to express contradictory opinions. In contrast, a rectangular table tends to solidify adversarial relationships by allowing the sides to sit opposite one another, as they do in negotiating sessions.

When attempting to impart information, for example, at a meeting with clients, are chairs set up classroom style, with rows all facing the speaker, implying your guests are there to listen? Or do you arrange for a more casual seating plan, one that allows interaction? A less formal atmosphere can encourage conversation.

Spatial Distance

The effectiveness of communication is determined in part by spatial distance—the distance separating those carrying on a conversation or the physical location of people who need to communicate in the course of their jobs. Whether a communication is delivered in person or at arm's length, the cultural implications of space between speakers and of lag time between replies to transmissions of information influence communication.

In *The Hidden Dimension,* Edward T. Hall discusses what people from different cultures consider to be a comfortable distance for conversation. He notes that Americans stand closer together when conversing than do the British and Germans; Arabs and Japanese stand closer together than do Americans. If you violate these rules, you run the risk of making the person you are talking with uncomfortable and thus less likely to listen carefully to what you are saying. Also, some distances for interaction are considered to be standard. For example, from actually touching to standing a foot and a half apart is usually considered intimate space, from that distance to 4 feet apart is personal space, social space goes up to 12 feet apart, and any space larger than that is public space.[16]

Distance poses another kind of problem in the workplace. Because people communicate most with those physically closest to them, people who are assembled in groups to work on special projects but spend most of their time in their usual workplaces tend to communicate less. Thomas Allen of MIT notes that "beyond a distance of 25 or 30 yards, personal interaction drops off markedly."[17] That is why it is important for management to try to bring together as much as possible those who work together.

People vary the space between themselves and those they are communicating with depending on the kind of message that they are delivering. In fact, the more comfortable you feel and the more you like an individual, the more likely you are to look that person in the eye during a conversation. But many people are uncomfortable delivering bad news in person. They prefer to send a letter, to have a third party intercede on their behalf, or even to call the individual on the telephone rather than being the bearer of bad news and having to watch the reactions.

Timing in Speech Patterns

In an article in *Psychology Today*, Albert Mehrabian discusses the effects of timing in speech patterns on communication. He says that most people always use the same timing—pauses between questions and answers, length of statements, timing between sentences, numbers and kinds of interruptions—when speaking. You can learn these patterns and use that information to improve your communication with an individual. For example, if you know someone will interrupt you with questions or comments frequently, you can construct your presentation with enough breaks to minimize the interruptions.

Mehrabian also points out that most people limit their statements to a length of about 30 seconds. However, when a person talks to someone with higher status, "the more the high-status person nods his head, the longer the speaker's utterances become. If the high-status person changes his own customary speech pattern toward longer or shorter utterances, the lower-status person will change his own speech in the same direction. If the high-status person often interrupts the speaker, or creates long silences, the speaker is likely to become quite uncomfortable."[18]

Adjusting to Cultural Differences

The global marketplace, a concept Theodore Levitt of the Harvard Business School first popularized in the 1970s, has a great deal to do with effective communication. As more and more companies market their services abroad, people who disregard nuances among cultures may not only find themselves being misunderstood but may also find themselves severely offending people they deal with in other parts of the world. Distance between speakers, as noted earlier, is one example of cultural differences affecting communications. Other important differences to take into account are choice of words and unconscious signals, such as body language.

To help ensure that your messages are understood, choose words or phrases that have few alternative meanings. For example, some phrases are often confusing, such as "he took the words right out of her mouth"; "it's a real rat race"; "it's a slap in the face"; "they really missed the boat." Use standard English, avoiding slang and figures of speech. In addition, be careful to avoid specialized language that requires people to have a common background or common interests to understand each other. This language includes sports terms ("time out," "ballpark figure," "out in left field") or military terms ("run a tight ship," "they did an about-face").

Cultural differences in the interpretation of common words can also cause confusion. For example, "no" is not a polite word in Latin America; thus, to avoid using it, particularly with a friend or colleague, a Latin American will say "yes" and later on explain why it cannot be done. In Japan "yes" means "I hear what you say." It does not mean "I will do it" or "I agree." The differences can be extreme: In Bulgaria, a shake of the head means yes; a nod, no.[19]

Furthermore, as just noted, the differences go deeper than spoken language. Body language must be learned anew. An article in *Public Relations Journal* notes:

> The American A-OK gesture, with thumb and forefinger touching in a circle, for example, means money to the Japanese, zero to the French, and an obscenity to Brazilians. . . . Arabs point or beckon as a way to summon dogs, so they don't appreciate that gesture for people. . . . Study such formalities as shaking hands. Most Europeans, for example, shake hands every time they see each other; several times a day is not unusual. If you ignore this formality, estranged feelings—or worse—can result.[20]

Finally, you don't even have to be present in a room with foreign visitors in order to offend them. According to Letitia Baldrige, Jacqueline Kennedy's White House chief of staff, "Never give an Argentinian a set of knives, as it signals a desire to cut off the business relationship. . . . Do not bring an Arab liquor or wine. It would be confiscated by customs since alcohol is illegal in an Islamic country. Do not bring food either, as it can be construed as a criticism of your host's hospitality. . . . Never give a clock to the Chinese, since it is a symbol of death."[21]

Another way to offend those of other cultures is to use stereotypes that have negative connotations; describing clothes with a Japanese influence as making the wearer look "geisha-like" instead of "modest" will offend many.[22] A few years ago, in the middle of an international debt crisis, the *Economist,* a respected British magazine, aroused a storm of protest when, to illustrate the Mexican debt problem, it pictured on its cover a figure in a sombrero on a donkey. Those in other cultures are quick to perceive all the negative connotations implicit in these stereotypes.

Successful communication with those in other cultures really requires two things: an awareness that cultural habits affect perception and devotion to the clearest, least convoluted way of expressing ideas. The last is essential in every kind of communication, not just cross-cultural communication.

Emphasize Clear and Uncluttered Communication

The need to communicate in the clearest possible fashion is critical. An article in *Personnel Journal* recounted the tale of a disabled worker who wrote to his company's benefits office to find out if he had to continue paying the premiums on his health insurance coverage. He received the following letter in response to his inquiry:

> Dear Mr. Larsen:
>
> Waiver of premium payments under your policy requires completion and submission of form H-404 by physician in attendance. Attestation properly notarized as to extent insured is disabled is required as total disability constitutes legal justification for activation of disability benefit provision in your policy.

Mr. Larsen returned the letter with the following message written across the bottom: "To whom it may concern: If you'd only tell me what this letter says and what you want me to do, you know I'd be happy to do it."[23]

This is just one of a number of problems that result from the failure to use clear, uncluttered language. The problems often involve a failure to think things through, to determine what adverse affects can arise when you do not always keep your listeners in mind.

Exclusionary Language

Many professions have a language all their own. Doctors communicate with other doctors about the health of their patients, attorneys confer with other attorneys about the complexities of their cases, technologists talk to other technologists about developing and installing new systems. As long as they talk to others within their profession, communication flows freely.

Problems occur when these and other professionals become so absorbed in their own world that they cannot or do not want to change their communication patterns to accommodate people outside their own narrow worlds.

Some people use jargon because they feel it makes them look more important; some feel that they can show others how smart they are by using language others don't understand. Some people, rather arrogantly, assume that if they know a specialized language, others should learn enough of it to understand them. And then there are those who hide behind their jargon; they feel most comfortable using that language, even if it is not appropriate for every audience. What these people do not realize is how often listeners tune out the minute they hear a term they do not understand.

No matter why people use language that others cannot understand, the results are the same. A wonderful example of poor communication appeared in an article warning people to avoid using unclear, jargon-laden language:

> Not being convinced, however, that theoretical lucidity is necessarily enhanced by terminological ponderosity, we shall avoid as much as possible, the use of the sort of jargon for which both sociologists and phenomenologists have acquired dubious notoriety.[24]

Context

Another factor that contributes to poor communication is a lack of information. Basing an opinion or judgment on bits and pieces of information without knowing prior events or whether there is information that would give those activities real meaning creates problems. Whether the fault is poor listening or poor communication on the part of the speaker is unimportant. For example, we yell at Johnny for hitting his sister. What we fail to realize is that seconds earlier, she hit him when we did not notice. One of the ways to improve communication is to present new audiences with enough background material to make sure they know the basics. In a meeting, it can make the difference between holding and losing an audience. If people do not understand why you have come to a certain conclusion, they can become so absorbed in trying to figure out how you reached it that they stop listening—or they may interrupt you to argue from a different frame of reference.

In addition, when you look at an event in isolation, without drawing a comparison or using other relevant cases as benchmarks, you will very likely miss the point. When the accounting professor asked the student whether achieving 45 percent profit growth last year was considered extraordinary growth for a company, the student replied "yes." What he failed to take into account was that all the other companies in the same industry sector achieved 68 percent profit growth, which makes the growth of the company the student thought was doing well pale by comparison.

Lastly, what is said takes on different meanings depending on why it is said and who is saying it. Let's say a new researcher says you should emphasize the company's new software address book program in the forthcoming sales effort aimed at selling programming packages. If you checked the survey the researcher conducted, you would discover that you should throw out its results. The survey was limited to 50 calls made to homes in an affluent suburb between 1:00 P.M. and 3:00 P.M. The question asked was, "If you had a home computer, which of the following programs would you be most interested in: a. games   b. tax returns   c. address book." What would the results have been if the same question had been asked when schoolchildren were more likely to answer? If the question had been asked only if callers said they had a computer? If the calls were made to owners of small businesses?[25]

Words and Phrases with Double Meanings

> I know that you believe you understand what you think I said, but
> I am not sure you realize that what you heard is not what I meant.
> —Anonymous

Many times communication barriers develop because you assume that the same words or phrases will have the same meaning for every member of an audience. As a good communicator, you should know that different people in an audience may hear the same message in different ways. This happens because they have different viewpoints, backgrounds, personal interests, education, experiences, and are in different levels within an organization. One way to help an audience reach a common understanding of a message is either to summarize the main points you are trying to make or to ask questions about your main message.

The following anecdote is a good example of this kind of mis-communication. Johnny and his mother went up to a cashier to pay their dinner bill, and Johnny saw after-dinner mints in a bowl next to the register. When he asked for one, his mother told him he could have a mint as long as he used the spoon that was in the bowl. Johnny reached into the bowl, put a mint on the spoon, and then put the spoon in his mouth.

Sarcasm

When people use sarcasm or humor to make a point, they leave themselves open to misunderstanding—especially with a foreign audience. When you use sarcasm,

> the information transmitted vocally contradicts the information transmitted verbally. Usually the verbal information is positive and the vocal negative . . . when vocal information contradicts verbal, vocal wins out. If someone calls you honey in a nasty tone of voice, you are likely to feel disliked: it is also possible to say "I hate you" in a way that conveys exactly the opposite meaning.[26]

Clearly, this is a problem if the person to whom the sarcasm is addressed does not understand that you are being sarcastic; it is always better to avoid sarcasm in your communications.

Emotion

Have you ever listened to two emotional people arguing across a conference table about who is right and who is wrong? As an independent third party, after 20 minutes of debate you probably thought, "If they would only stop and listen to each other, rather than trying to prove that they are right, they would realize that they are basically saying the same thing."

When people are in a heated debate and put their blinders on, the only way to get them to stop and think is for a facilitator to ask each to find the merit in what the other is saying before they continue presenting their arguments.

Management Intimidation

Another way the communications process and flow of ideas can be hindered is for management to present its ideas before others have had a chance to speak. After listening to a confident presentation of an idea by a superior, subordinates have a much more difficult time responding to requests for their ideas; they think that the superior will consider any suggestion an attack. Communications suffer just as much if management always finds fault with the ideas presented, never offering compliments for suggestions made in good faith.

Conclusion

It has been said that "one advantage of talking to yourself is that you know at least someone is listening"—and understands what you are saying. That's a pretty sad commentary on life. And it is even more applicable in business, where so much that you need to know comes clothed in forms that make it almost impossible to understand.

A good way of thinking about the problem of communication is to return to the comparison between business and fighting a war. Can you imagine an English-speaking general trying to lead troops onto a battlefield with a sergeant who only speaks French; a lieutenant, Spanish; and the rank-and-file, Italian? The army would be in a state of chaos, or at least at a major disadvantage. All the time the soldiers should devote to planning strategies for winning battles would be spent trying to understand one another.

It is no different in business. Developing relationships with people, both within and outside an organization, requires clear communication. Perhaps the best advice on listening was provided by Epictetus some 2,000 years ago: "We have two ears and one mouth, and should use them in that proportion."

11

Service Quality: Forethought, Not Afterthought

Service, according to Leon Gorman, president of L. L. Bean, is a "day-in, day-out, ongoing, never-ending, unremitting, persevering, compassionate type of activity."[1] Given L. L. Bean's position as a leader in quality of service in its industry, the message is one you cannot afford to ignore. Indeed, your worst nightmare should be overhearing a client say:

- "They're getting too big and don't care about us anymore."
- "We're a large client and our business is still taken for granted."
- "I know they're in business to make money, but it would be nice if they cared a little about our needs too."
- "I have no complaints about their product—it's excellent—but service doesn't seem to be one of their priorities."
- "I can never get a question answered. No one solves my problems; they just pass them along."
- "You only get good service when you stay on top of them."

Why is service important? In a Forum Corporation survey of 2,374 customers from 14 organizations, more than 40 percent listed poor service as the number one reason for switching to the competition, while only 8 percent listed price.[2] To make matters worse, a Technical Assistance Research Programs study also says that the average person who has been burned by a firm tells nine to ten colleagues about that experience, and 13 percent of dissatisfied customers will spread the bad news to more than 20 people.[3] Moreover, the danger to your business of losing clients is critical: According to the study, it is easier and five times cheaper to keep an existing client than to recruit a new one.

Good service enhances your chances of attracting new clients through word of mouth, makes it easier for you to do business with existing clients, and promotes cross-selling opportunities (see Chapter 12, which contains a complete discussion of cross-selling). Furthermore, the Strategic Planning Institute's Profit Impact for Marketing Strategy (PIMS) database reveals that companies rated highly by their customers for service charge on average 9 percent more than those rated poorly.[4] Clearly, low prices are less important to buyers than quality service.

In the past, when management in some manufacturing companies discovered that a product did not live up to the organization's quality standards, it added inspectors to the production line to find defective parts, thus raising the level of quality. Other companies dealt with the problem by building quality into their products through improved design. Thus, rather than spending time, money, and effort locating defects after the fact, successful companies eliminated them up front.

This solution is analogous to many client-retention programs, which are designed to keep dissatisfied clients from switching to other firms. If those same clients were treated properly in the first place, a firm could spend more time developing innovative ways to respond to their needs rather than getting caught in a turnstile of finding new clients, trying to save relationships, then again having to get new clients.

The reasons for the lack of quality service are manifold. Too many organizations are burdened by levels of approval, pass-the-buck bureaucracy, poor administrative support, and excessive turnover of personnel. As a result, their employees are often rude, misinformed, inexperienced, and apathetic; employees do not understand the company's products and services, they fail to understand deadlines, and then exhibit a condescending "You're lucky I'm helping you" attitude. Moreover, employees ignore clients because they are rushing to and from internal meetings or dealing with problems that do not affect their clients.

Karl Albrecht summed up this problem in *At America's Service:*

> Through the fault of no one in particular, the arthritic organization has evolved to an internal state of affairs that places compliance over sense, policy above people, rules above reason. This makes it difficult for people to question and reexamine the ways they do things and to experiment with new ways that may be more effective.[5]

If your organization seems to have such problems, where should you begin? The Band-Aid approach—new slogans, advertising the problem away, smile training, or program of the month—does not compensate for inadequacies. In other words, the changes you make must be more than on the surface. Albrecht makes the point by retelling a story: "Abraham Lincoln had a favorite riddle he liked to spring on people. He used to ask 'How many legs does a dog have, if you call the tail a leg?' When the unsuspecting respondent would answer 'five' Lincoln would chastise, 'No, he has four. Calling his tail a leg doesn't make it a leg.' "[6]

Selling Is Essential for Getting New Business; Service Is Essential for Keeping It

One way you can tackle the problem of poor service is to try to determine its scope—how extensive is the problem, what are its roots, how does it manifest itself? To determine the size of the problem you are facing, you must evaluate your organization as honestly as possible:

- Is your organization willing to make policy changes to make your life or a client's life better?
- Does your firm tend to take clients for granted because they've been clients for a long time?

- Do your firm's employees do their best work *only after* the competition has made inroads?
- Do your firm's employees know that their first and foremost job is to service clients?
- Are your firm's policies geared to the long-term success of your clients or only to your firm's quick profits?
- How well do you really understand your clients' businesses? How much do they know about yours?
- Do you know why clients are happy or unhappy with your firm's services? What steps have you taken to find out?
- Are you accessible when your clients need you?
- In what areas do you treat your clients differently now that you have them as clients than you did when you were courting them?
- Are you so concerned about losing your clients that you stop making innovative suggestions?
- Do you encourage and reward employee performance that is in the best interest of clients?

Service—the Only Real Product

To be successful, to attract new business and encourage repeat business, your firm must offer more than a basic product. Harvard University's Theodore Levitt developed a framework for differentiating products and services. He used the framework to describe the progression from the generic product to the potential product; this progression illuminates the need to continuously develop and improve the services provided to clients.[7]

- *The generic product.* This is the bare bones of what you must have to be in business. Just as you must pass the bar to be an attorney, get your C.P.A. to be a certified accountant or your M.D. to be a doctor, own planes to run an airline, you must have a product that attracts a customer to be in business.
- *The expected product.* Customers have expectations that exceed the generic product. Price, delivery, technical support, tim-

ing, quality, return policy, service availability both in terms of employees who can answer questions and replacement parts, and so forth, are some ways in which potential customers decide which company they will buy from.

- *The augmented product.* This is what you have when your firm provides customers, on a voluntary basis, with more than they think they need, more than they expect. Augmented products are those extras that your firm provides to differentiate itself from the competition. Not all benefits are considered equal in the eyes of the beholder, because everyone's needs are not identical. For example, adding a designer label increases costs—a small consideration to a customer willing to pay more to achieve status but of little value to one whose critical concern is holding down costs.

  Augmentation is a two-way street. As time passes, expectations begin to vary depending on use, need, and competitive offerings. Furthermore, expectations can be raised because everyone selling that product or service has augmented it in the same way. The expected product becomes what was once an augmented product. For example, Sears has found itself having to make sales, once infrequent events, everyday occurrences; car manufacturers are rapidly being locked into offering rebates because they have become an expected part of the deal.

- *The potential product.* Levitt says, "What you have done refers to the augmented product; what remains to be done refers to the potential—everything potentially feasible to attract and hold customers."[8]

To market your product or service successfully, you must focus attention on the augmented and potential product. By determining your customers' needs, anticipating their desires, augmenting your service, and continually improving, you will better satisfy your clients now and in the future.

The relationship between your clients' needs and your ability to provide services to fill those needs is best illustrated in Figure 11.1. Service excellence is achieved when your firm is most able to deliver those services that are of highest importance to your client. The greatest problem in service relationships comes from

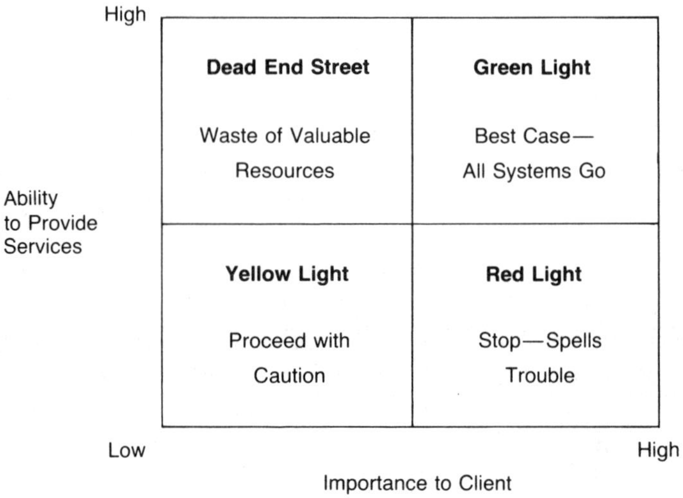

High ┌─────────────────┬─────────────────┐
     │   │   │
     │ **Dead End Street** │   **Green Light**   │
     │   │   │
     │ Waste of Valuable │   Best Case—   │
     │   Resources   │ All Systems Go │
     │   │   │
     ├─────────────────┼─────────────────┤
     │   │   │
     │ **Yellow Light**   │   **Red Light**   │
     │   │   │
     │ Proceed with   │ Stop—Spells   │
     │   Caution   │   Trouble   │
     │   │   │
     └─────────────────┴─────────────────┘

Vertical axis label (left): Ability to Provide Services — High at top, Low at bottom.

Horizontal axis label (below): Importance to Client — Low at left, High at right.

Figure 11.1

being ineffective in areas important to your client. Being ineffective in areas not important to your client is not much of a risk; for example, insurance agents who cannot provide estate planning to their clients do not have a problem if their markets consist primarily of young singles who come to them for apartment and automobile insurance. But keep in mind that things change; for example, as those agents' clients age, being ineffective in those areas may become a problem. Finally, having a high ability to provide services that are relatively unimportant to your clients is a waste of your firm's valuable resources.

Marketing Customer Satisfaction, Not Just Products

Berry, Parasuraman, and Zeithaml conducted a study[9] that attempted to answer the question "What do service customers desire?" They surveyed people in the retail banking, bank credit card, product repair, and long-distance telephone industries. By so doing, they were able to identify five dimensions of service quality:

- *Tangibles.* The physical facilities, equipment, appearance of personnel. In *A Passion for Excellence,* Tom Peters and Nancy Austin relate that "Don Burr, President of People Express, once said that coffee stains on the flip-down trays [in the airplane] mean [to the passengers] that we do our maintenance wrong."[10] You should be able to answer "Yes" to these questions: When marketing advertising, legal, or consulting services, do you take extra care in packaging your recommendations? Are your presentations professionally prepared? Are your reports free of typos and grammatical errors? When you are selling a service, remember that because of the intangible nature of your product, these tangibles represent the caliber of your work.

- *Reliability.* The ability to perform the desired service dependably, accurately, and consistently. Do you promise only what you can deliver? Do you manage the large as well as the small details? This is critical because firms and individuals are often tested in areas that are of minimal strategic significance or political sensitivity or that are of less monetary value until they prove reliable—only then are they given larger, more significant assignments.

- *Responsiveness.* The willingness to provide prompt service and help to clients. Do you refuse to take calls from clients after-hours or to serve people because the way they are dressed makes you think they will be unable to meet your fees? Do you ignore secretaries' requests for assistance because you think they're too far down the totem pole? Such behavior becomes a cause for resentment and builds a reputation for unresponsiveness.

- *Assurance.* Employees' knowledge, courtesy, and ability to convey trust and confidence. Are your employees encouraged to keep learning so that they remain current in their field? Do they practice their presentations on clients or rehearse enough to come across as thoroughly knowledgeable? Do they demonstrate their objectivity by presenting all the alternatives before making a recommendation?

- *Empathy.* Providing caring, individualized attention to clients. Does your firm go out of its way to provide free assistance to clients in other areas than the one you are retained for? Do you try to squeeze every penny out of clients, or, realizing that an activity took longer than it should have because of internal problems, do you voluntarily reduce the charge for it?

An evaluation of these aspects of service quality concluded that reliability was the most important dimension, regardless of the service being studied. Further examinations have shown that reliability is usually thought to be the weakest element of company performance—and the greatest source of service problems. Clearly, a firm that is failing to provide reliable service has a major customer relations problem, but the problem is far from unsolvable.

The Moment of Truth

In *At America's Service,* Karl Albrecht further clarified the term "moment of truth," which was first coined by SAS President Jan Carlzon as "any episode in which the customer comes into contact with any aspect of the organization and gets an impression of the quality of its service."[11] The first step is to make all employees at all levels aware that service is critical to a firm's success and that failure to provide it is frowned upon and initiatives to provide it are rewarded. For example, American Express encourages employee awareness of the importance of service quality through an annual "great performers award" for employees who provide high levels of service.

When that kind of attitude permeates a company, success follows. Take the story of a corporate executive whose company travel office always gives, on his orders, preference to one particular hotel chain. The executive has never forgotten the night years ago when he arrived at a Los Angeles hotel after a coast-to-coast flight at the end of a number of weeks of extensive travel. At the hotel's registration desk he was told that his room was not yet ready even though it was well after check-in time. The desk clerk called over an assistant manager, who apologized and escorted the weary traveler to the hotel's best restaurant. There he told the maître d' to look after the executive. When he returned to the desk after finishing his complimentary dinner, the executive was told his room was available and that his first night's stay was on the house. He has kept a favorable impression of that hotel chain ever since then—and acted on it.

Too many firms forget that they are always performing a balancing act—that they are judged on numerous factors, including the impression people have of their company both in the period leading up to the sale and after the sale is made. That is why it is critical that all details, no matter how insignificant they seem to be, be well managed at every level. Remember that your organization will be judged by its address, the impression its lobby gives, the way telephone calls are handled, the quality of presentations, its advertisements, and the quality of the services at every level from billing to service calls.

Be careful that no one in your firm believes that the final deliverable or end product is the *only* basis for measuring quality service. After all, as a consumer, would you dine at a restaurant that served excellent food on dirty plates and provided lousy service? Would you deposit your savings in a bank that continually made you wait in long lines or made mistakes on your monthly statements? Would you shop in a store that took four weeks to get a part and two service people on two separate occasions to fix a product? Would you retain a consultant who, although clearly brilliant, submitted a proposal filled with grammatical errors and typos?

It is critical that all details, no matter how insignificant they seem, be managed. Your salespeople must be knowledgeable, prompt, and reliable and so must the administrative group that runs the organization. Your final report for a client must be thorough, organized, and professional. The executive interviews you conducted to collect the data you used for the report should have been the same. The clients reading the report will remember if the interviews were filled with appointment cancellations and conducted by unprepared, inexperienced interviewers.

The next time around clients remember everything that came before and that occurred after the sale. Remind everyone in your organization that not only must you sell and service the car, but you must also service the client.

The Road to Enhanced Customer Relationships

In *Telephone: The First One Hundred Years,* John Brooks pointed out that "talking to customers tends to counteract the most self-destructive habit of great corporations, that of talking to themselves."[12] Therein lies the first step in solving your quality service problems—making sure that you know the needs of your clients. This requires adopting a philosophy of focusing externally. Internal focus usually results from ego ("I've been in the business for so long I know what the client wants")—from management that hides in ivory towers and has little contact with clients, from too many management levels with communication flowing downward, and from management that just does not listen to its own people, those on the front lines.

In your daily dealings with clients and in your internal evaluation meetings, keep in mind the following rules:

- It is not enough to say that you care about your clients' needs—you must go out and find out what they are.
- It is not enough to respond to clients' demands—you must anticipate them.
- Ask not only how you are doing but also what else you could be doing.

Periodic evaluations are a first step to ensuring that quality service is part of your normal operation. These require getting out from behind your desk and discussing possible problems with some selected clients as well as with your own employees (and that involves the art of listening, not talking). Staying in your office and reading reports prepared by your senior management can keep you from learning about the problems that might not yet be affecting your profits. For example, John G. Smale, Procter & Gamble's chairman and chief executive, "listens to recordings of the company's toll-free customer hotline in his car."[13] This gives him a sense of how his employees relate to customers and of his customers' concerns.

You must also occasionally conduct formal evaluations. However, all your efforts to discover problems will be wasted if you then ignore what you have learned. The evaluation process should be structured to tell you what your reputation is among the people you deal with every day and to tell you what the general public, users, influencers, buyers, decision makers, former customers, and current customers think about your organization. The expense involved in conducting such surveys will be met by retained business, additional business from old clients, and business from new clients attracted to you because of your reputation for service.

Surveying clients can help you know exactly

- Why you win or lose clients.
- What kinds of service clients are actually receiving.
- What kinds of service they expect.
- What enhancements can be made.

Formal and informal surveys can consist of active listening, customer complaint analyses, employee suggestions, quarterly client account reviews, a hot line to a firm's president; interviews with customers, customers' customers, and suppliers; sales force call reports; customer advisory panels; and dealer panels. There are also more intensive methods. For example, you could set up focus groups, bringing in a series of clients and holding three- or four-hour sessions in which their current needs and plans for the future are discussed; such meetings can provide a great deal of information. Another method of evaluation is the use of mystery shoppers, the device many airlines use, hiring people to fly various routes and to assess every aspect of their operation, from ticketing to luggage handling to in-flight service and comfort.

Promise Less, Deliver More

If after performing such surveys, you conclude that your organization is having problems with service quality, you can take a number of steps. One of the basic rules, according to Berry, Parasuraman, and Zeithaml, is to remember that "customers assess service quality by comparing what they want or expect to what they actually get or perceive they are getting. To earn a reputation for quality, an organization must meet or exceed client expectations."[14]

As noted earlier, reliability, the most important dimension of service, involves avoiding making promises you cannot fill. Whether you say things to make clients feel good about you for the moment, exaggerate to win their business, or promise something that you cannot deliver (because it requires assistance from other colleagues or because you are an eternal optimist), you may be the hero today, but you will be a failure tomorrow. Ask yourself whether you have been guilty of making unrealistic claims.

- Have you claimed that your firm has "the very best investment track record in the industry," when past successes cannot guarantee future performance?
- Have you blithely—and hoping against hope that it is true—said, "We should have no problem getting you a sizable tax refund," without doing at least a preliminary calculation of figures?
- Have you claimed that a "press conference will lead to great visibility" when you have no guarantee that the media will view the event in the same light as you?

Be sure that you control the expectations your clients develop about what you can do for them. For example, in the 1988 presidential debates, George Bush stressed his opponent's experience as a debater, lowering the expectations about his own performance—expectations he was able to meet. Taking an example closer to home, senior management carefully guides Wall Street analysts expectations to ensure that their earnings estimates are reasonable, that they don't build expectations that their firms are unable to deliver.

You can manage expectation levels in a number of ways:

- Carefully examine the situation for all possible problems before making promises about timing (when the material will be delivered, when the project will be completed), costs, performance of the product or service.

- When marketing intangibles, fully describe your end product so clients know what they will receive (and can avoid surprises).
- If clients make changes that translate into additional costs, be sure to spell them out as they are incurred to minimize the shock when the bill arrives.
- Explain that delays in getting approval may translate into longer delays at the end of a project.
- When you know of delays or problems, don't wait till they compound, but bring them to clients' attention at the earliest possible moment. Clients must not, of course, be notified every time a problem occurs; you should use your best judgment. When clients are aware that a problem exists (but you are handling it), they are reassured. If, on the other hand, they discover the problem by themselves or from a third party, they may begin to doubt the whole relationship. They cannot help asking themselves, "What else is this person hiding from me?" By providing bad as well as good news, you establish greater credibility in the relationship.
- Be conservative in your estimates rather than promising the world each time and falling short on your promises.
- Don't be afraid to be human—to say you can't deliver when it's not possible.

Problems as Opportunities

Obviously, the greater control you have over a process, the greater the likelihood you will be able to meet expectations. Service problems are often caused by inadequate skills, too great a work load, varying priorities, lack of training, personnel problems, apathy, and no follow-up when you—the primary contact—are unavailable. It is up to you to insist that those responsible for follow-up be properly trained.

Part of servicing clients is the way that you deal with problems that arise. You can solve these problems and create goodwill in a number of ways:

- When a major problem surfaces, be careful that it does not overshadow smaller ones, which may be nagging away at your clients. Meet with clients while the big problems are being handled and make it clear that you want to know if anything else is not going as smoothly as expected. Clients might mention something small at the moment that can be dealt with immediately but that they had hesitated to bring up because they were afraid it would divert attention from major problems. This will give you the opportunity to show your concern and spare both you and your clients trouble down the line. It is always easier to solve problems when they are small.

- Forget who is to blame. Get to the heart of the problem and resolve it. Later, go back and correct the situation that led to the problem so that it doesn't occur again.

- Make sure you have a system for documenting problems to see if patterns emerge. Complaints should not be judged or screened. They should be viewed as opportunities to improve policies and procedures.

- When handling dissatisfied customers, start by dealing with them on an emotional level—empathize with your clients. Your initial goal is to calm down clients so you can gather facts by asking questions. Once you have the facts, begin to rebuild confidence by assuring clients that you will look into the problem and call them back. Customer complaints should be handled (or an update given on the status of the problem) within 24 hours.

Resolving problems provides a great opportunity to make clients feel they are important and their needs are being heard. The fact that you see that a service problem is resolved to their satisfaction leaves lasting impressions with your clients, making maintaining relationships easy. Your customers who have problems and complain to you about them are giving you an opportunity to keep them as clients. Surveys show that you can win back between 54 percent and 70 percent of these clients by resolving their complaints. Actually, about 95 percent of this group will become loyal customers again if their complaints are handled well and quickly.

But be careful; do not assume that the complaints you get are all that there are. According to a Technical Assistance Research Programs study, "on average 1 in 4 customers is unhappy enough with customer service to leave an organization. But of all those that are unhappy, 26 out of 27 will not complain."[15] A study by the U.S. Office of Consumer Affairs reveals that consumers don't complain for three reasons: 1) they believe complaining is a waste of their time and effort; 2) they believe complaining will not do any good (no one wants to hear about their problems); and 3) they do not know how to complain or where to lodge complaints.[16]

Clearly, it is important to develop mechanisms for identifying clients who are unhappy with the quality of service your firm delivers. That is why some companies spend a great deal of time and effort on publicizing their customer service units. General Electric is a leader in this area. It has set up the GE Answer Center, a toll-free, 24-hour-a-day, 7-day-a-week complaint and inquiry service that it advertises in print and broadcast media and publicizes in the literature provided with every purchase. The people manning the phones are well trained (they receive five weeks of training) and backed by technical specialists to whom they can pass along calls they cannot answer. In 1985 the Center handled about 2.6 million calls; about a third were prepurchase inquiries, a third concerned product use and care after purchase, and a third involved service. Only 5 percent of the calls could be classified as complaints.[17]

Organizations that consider customer satisfaction critical to their long-term success can set up a number of programs to remain close to customers. Few such programs, however, can match Nissan's recent $5 million customer satisfaction survey. Nissan hired a Chicago research organization to phone every new car buyer and each car owner who came in for warranty service to check on the service they received. This enabled the firm to resolve quickly any problems that were uncovered.

It is easy for any firm to set up such systems. Make frequent calls to see that everything is going well in the beginning of relationships; later on make occasional follow-up calls to ask if any problems have surfaced and if there is anything else you can do for your clients. You should periodically check with your service department to find out if your clients have had problems they haven't told you about. If you detect some cooling of relationships, it may be time for a survey or questionnaire—something that makes clients focus on their dissatisfaction or that provides them with an opportunity to express dissatisfaction without being confrontational. You must not only meet clients' expectations, you must see to it that they continue to be met. Remember that if you do not hear about problems firsthand, you have not instilled trust in your clients. That is a problem you must remedy immediately.

Treating the Client as a Long-term Asset

Do you view your business relationship in terms of one transaction, or do you view it in terms of the potential business that you could receive if you properly manage a relationship over the years? The difference in mind-set will certainly guide the policy decisions that your organization makes. Always assume that at some point you will get paid back for everything you do for clients; it may be by word-of-mouth referral or additional business, but it will happen.

Perhaps the clearest evidence of a firm's mind-set comes from its employees. A recent article in the *Wall Street Journal* noted that "in Japan employees tend to look on their jobs as careers. . . . They are promised lifetime employment, and promotions are made from within. . . . Probably as a result, [they] seem to be more methodical and make fewer mistakes than their American counterparts. When they do goof, they bend over backwards to make amends."[18]

Does your firm ask employees to perform in such a way that they are all working toward the goal of satisfying clients? Management practices should be constructed to improve service, not stifle it. Be careful that your firm's emphasis is on long-term, not short-term, performance. No employee of your firm should ever hear these statements: "Don't resolve their problems—go out and get more business"; "Go over the heads of your client contacts— it's taking too long to get a decision"; "Don't spend time with clients after they buy, find new prospects."

Firms should shift from an internal to an external perspective. For example, one Pennsylvania bank asks employees to fill out deposit slips with Vaseline smeared on their glasses or to count money with their fingers taped together. The idea is to give them a better understanding of what older customers with glaucoma or arthritis may go through when they're in the bank.[19]

The critical importance of quality service to a firm's future must be strongly communicated to employees. First, senior management must set the proper example by realizing the signals that it sends. Second, employees should be brought together to discuss service quality, which must be incorporated into orientation and training programs, be made part of the performance appraisal system, and be promoted through proper role models, internal video programs, newsletters, ceremonies, and rituals.

Employee performance should be continually monitored and rewarded against preset standards. Ask yourself if you are getting new business from existing clients and reducing turnover among existing clients. Such measures, and such concern for employee-client relationships, are often not part of a corporate culture. In *A Passion for Excellence,* Austin and Peters noted that in a seminar with 40 company presidents, "everyone present—40 out of 40—[said] that long-term customer satisfaction was priority number one. Then they asked a follow-up question. How many of you measure any of your people directly on a third-party or impartial quantitative in-house measure of long-term total customer satisfaction? The answer was zero."[20]

Contrast that with the behavior of American Express, which is noted for service quality and, as noted earlier, rewards its employees for providing it. American Express publishes an annual summary of service quality for employees and has over 100 programs for recognizing and rewarding people who take care of customers. In the same way, the GE Answer Center has a built-in evaluation process that includes call monitoring, surveys of customers who have called in, and rewards for good work.[21] And Nordstrom, a 68-year-old retailing firm whose department stores have a reputation for excellence, honors exceptional salespeople with cash, discounts, and membership in its "pace-setters" club. Moreover, to encourage employees to provide exceptional service, they "are given the freedom to do almost anything to satisfy shoppers." In response to that mandate, one saleswoman delivered stockings to a frantic businesswoman's office before a big meeting.[22]

All for One—One for All

The authors of the book *Service Quality* sum up what it takes to provide service excellence as follows:

> Service excellence comes from a chemistry of leadership, solid information, organizational infrastructure, good people who are free to serve, technology that supports their efforts. . . . Service excellence is heart not just think, execution not just strategy, little ideas not just big ideas. It is the marshalling of resources—human and otherwise—it is a well-designed service system.[23]

All employees must accept responsibility for servicing clients. Offices, divisions, functional areas, and geographic locations must be coordinated to see that all clients are properly served. Clients will not have a favorable image of an organization that sends three different representatives to call on them in a week, that improperly bills them, that has employees who have not heard of services they ask about, that cannot locate the proper individual to answer their questions, that makes them frequently wait to have their phone calls answered, and that allows them to be told different stories about the same product in different locations.

Avoiding these problems takes a commitment to service quality as the road to building long-term customer relationships—and it can be brought about through proper internal communications. When everyone in the firm—for example, marketing, service, and administration—works together, problems that adversely affect the organization's image can be easily resolved so that it can win a reputation for service quality.

12

The Power of
Cross-Selling

While in the bank to make a deposit, a customer asks the teller if the bank sells life insurance. Without glancing up from stamping the deposit slips and clearly uninterested, the teller says he doesn't think so. As the customer walks out of the bank, she notices a large sign in the window saying "See Us About Savings Bank Life Insurance."

The customer, curious about what is available and a little annoyed at having been brushed off, goes back into the bank and finds the assistant manager. It takes her a few minutes to discover that the bank officer knows little about the service: He does nothing more than give the customer a business card with a telephone number on it. When called, the telephone contact apologizes for having run out of marketing literature, but promises to send some information. When it arrives some weeks later, it turns out to be an almost illegible copy of a rate table.

Needless to say, the bank customer buys her life insurance elsewhere. The bank lost an opportunity to increase business because it had not trained and encouraged its employees in *cross-selling*—selling additional products or services to existing or inactive customers. This bank is far from the only organization that is not taking advantage of opportunities to cross-sell. All types of organizations forget that by marketing throughout a buyer's organization—horizontally to other functional areas, vertically to those on higher or lower hierarchical levels, and to other locations, divisions, subsidiaries, or product areas—sales can be increased dramatically for far less expenditure of time and money than it takes to acquire new clients. In fact, as discussed in Chapter 11, it is easier and five times cheaper to sell to existing clients than to recruit new ones.

Why Cross-Selling?

Everyone in your organization should understand that cross-selling is a "win-win" situation, offering benefits to both your clients, the buyers, and your firm, the seller. Your clients save time because they deal with fewer vendors and work with someone familiar with the needs of their organizations. Instead of spending a good deal of time and money developing additional business outside, you can concentrate on servicing accounts, nurturing relationships, and finding new opportunities to expand business with current clients.

In fact, the seller who identifies clients' needs *before* they begin shopping for other firms preempts the competition and has a better chance of being in the enviable position of a "sole source." In this situation, the seller does not have to discount products or services unduly, allowing the firm to maintain its full profit margins. The financial advantage of cross-selling was noted by John Costigan, vice president for business growth of CIGNA, a large insurance company, who said that in 1987 "CIGNA spent less than $300,000 to produce some $352 million in cross-selling revenue, or less than 0.1 percent of sales."[1]

If an organization hopes to take advantage of these benefits, opportunities for cross-selling must be exploited deliberately as a matter of policy. To be effective, however, cross-selling not only needs management support and a workable organizational structure, it also requires a frame of mind in which every sale or transaction is regarded as the beginning of a new sales opportunity, not the culmination of an old one. Remember that the essence of cross-selling is building and leveraging long-term relationships. These are best developed by a passion for service excellence and a belief in continuous development, no matter what the industry—from banking to beverages, from consulting to construction.

Barriers to Successful Cross-Selling

Even though the benefits of cross-selling seem clear, many companies and individuals spend a great deal of time looking for new business prospects and ignoring the opportunities that can be found in their own backyards. Any company that wants to expand business opportunities with existing clients has to recognize these opportunities and understand how to pursue them.

If your firm is missing opportunities, it may be because entrenched company attitudes, structures, and policies are counterproductive. For instance, the following are typical barriers to cross-selling in many firms:

- *Pressure to produce immediate results.* Too many organizations suffer from the "What have you done for me today?" syndrome. Because they are not properly motivated to spend the time to build long-standing relationships, employees often ignore sales opportunities that require additional selling time or long lead times. The goal in such firms is always the quick sale.

- *Lack of incentive.* Employees are neither encouraged nor rewarded for promoting the entire product line to every client. As a result, they have a "Why should I bother?" attitude.

- *Improper role modeling.* The organization rewards those who excel in their primary job functions, even though they may make no contribution to the company's overall efforts.

- *Inadequate employee orientation.* The organization confirms the activities already listed by training employees in their primary roles only and not encouraging a broad viewpoint. Thus, islands of workers have single, isolated views of the company. They should instead all work together to achieve a common objective.

- *Limited sales skills.* Employees do not know how to identify client needs and translate them into opportunities or benefits in order to promote new products and services.

- *Custom-made products.* If every product or service is custom-made for each client, it is difficult to train employees to identify new business opportunities with other clients. It is also difficult to develop promotional materials to communicate firmwide product capabilities to others.

- *Contacts made at too low a level.* Client contacts do not have the power or understanding to make decisions across company lines. Their scope of responsibility is so narrowly defined that they focus exclusively on their own immediate needs.

- *Inadequate information systems.* Client information is difficult to obtain, inaccurate, or presented in an untimely or unusable format. The sales force has to rely on personal communication with others in the company and with outside contacts for basic information, which wastes time and energy. If you know whom to call and what those clients have already purchased, you start one step ahead.

- *Launching new products haphazardly.* Clients of firms with no formal policy or overall strategy for introducing new services may never find out that those services exist.

- *No defined sales territories.* Clients are not assigned dedicated employee contacts but are assigned to salespeople randomly when they call a central number. This prevents the formation of broad and deep customer-supplier relationships.

- *Sales territories that are too broad.* When your territory can best be described as "the world," it is easier to mass market and follow up on leads than to focus on one client and try to maximize sales efforts in that organization. Some companies try to get around this problem by establishing key or major account programs to focus efforts.

- *Sales territories are frequently changed.* If an organization moves people around, reorganizes frequently, or does not have a tenure system for its sales territories, people hesitate to concentrate on building long-term relationships. Instead, they devote their efforts to making as many sales as quickly as possible. They have no motivation for building relationships that will result in future sales when they know they will not be handling those accounts for very long.

- *Revolving-door relationships.* Quick promotions and excessive personnel turnover discourage long-term relationships, making selling additional products and services to an existing account less likely.

- *Lack of cross-selling information.* Employees are not informed that a product delivered to a client's East Coast facility can apply to another one elsewhere. (Successful selling to a parent company often can be expanded to include selling to a subsidiary as well.)

Six Requirements for Successful Cross-Selling

The most important step in breaking down these barriers to cross-selling is to assign cross-selling the priority it deserves; it should not become a program of the month but must become part of a firm's culture. It cannot be something dealt with by occasional attacks, for example, by issuing brochures every few years to explain the different services a firm provides. Moreover, if you do not keep employees up-to-date on new products or services but offer them compensation for selling new services as part of a reward system, frustration and resentment build when they miss opportunities to cross-sell because they did not have enough information about the service or the reasons why customers would be interested.

It is thus critical that all parts of an organization be involved in the effort to cross-sell, from management to training to systems to marketing. To do this, it is necessary to set up a cross-selling effort that includes as basic elements a management philosophy, personal qualities, education and training, incentives, information systems, and internal and external communications.

Management Philosophy

Cross-selling flourishes most in firms in which top management is deeply concerned with satisfying its current clients and places a greater value on its long-term position in the marketplace than on short-term results. Such a firm tends to be market-driven, basing its products and services on the needs of its clients rather than trying to force-feed them the services it has on hand. This kind of firm invests significantly in research and development, as well as in market research and client support. It works continuously to improve every aspect of its operations. For example, it would rather build quality into its products through improvements in design than spend time, money, and effort locating defects after the fact. It would rather delay production if a product does not live up to its quality standards than add inspectors to a production line to find defective parts. In other words, it maintains customer relationships not by reacting to complaints but by fixing the systems that lead to complaints.

The first step in building this kind of mind-set is for top management to make cross-selling part of its corporate culture. As part of that commitment, it must promote cross-selling and ask for a similar commitment from everyone at every level in the entire organization. Top management, illustrating its emphasis on cross-selling, should be included in both planning and executing the cross-selling effort.

An organization that cross-sells successfully inspires an esprit de corps among its employees. It is a firm in which employees are encouraged to work together to achieve organizational objectives. Barriers are broken down between functional departments, business units, and company locations so that policies and procedures are not developed for the convenience of employees but for their overall impact on client service.

A firm that cross-sells successfully also works to build a spirit of teamwork among employees and breaks down barriers to communications between individuals. It encourages new employees to meet colleagues not directly involved in the group into which they were hired and fosters the building of bonds among its employees, thus promoting both loyalty to the firm and loyalties within and between groups.

Moreover, this kind of firm encourages networking between its offices and different divisions (deposits, insurance, loans in a bank; audit, tax, consulting in a professional services firm; acquisitions, production, and distribution in a publishing house) in order to foster relations between employees and to build general awareness of the services that each group provides.

In addition, the firm believes that it is important to keep its lines of communication open, for example, through an in-house newsletter, a mechanism for making suggestions, and regular, informal gatherings of staff. It also continually tries to encourage an awareness of what the organization is about and a feeling of cooperation among its employees. To minimize turnover, which destroys the bonds built between suppliers and buyers, the firm emphasizes everyone's importance, playing up teamwork and diminishing the star system. Basically, an "everybody-sells" philosophy is reinforced from the president on down to everyone within the organization.

As part of its efforts, the firm recruits new employees selectively and devotes adequate resources to their training and development. It believes that because it is going to make a major investment in its employees, it must find the right people. This is a philosophy of not hiring bodies on the assumption that they can be discarded or replaced quickly. The firm believes that high turnover costs organizations dearly and that employees who leave the organization take part of it with them, if only in the loss of established relationships.

Once it finds the people who can contribute to the organization, it will train them not just to do their own job but to understand the full scope of the organization—to know what the firm does at every level and in every division and how it fits into the industry it is a part of. It will make every effort to ensure that these investments are not lost.

Successful firms also make sure that employees are regularly given sufficient time to deepen their knowledge about the services they sell and to remain up-to-date in their fields. Employees then understand applications as well as theory and are able to see beyond their own particular area of expertise.

When a firm does all that, it ensures that its employees identify with the organization's clients, that they understand the business issues that affect them, and that they can anticipate new ways to help their clients in the future. Take the case of a computer software company that has been encouraging its employees to have training sessions every Monday morning. The first part of these sessions is devoted to reinforcing selling skills, the second part to new product announcements and new product applications—and recognition of employees for outstanding service.

Recently, an employee of that software company was helping a new client learn the application at the client's office. Someone from the client's accounting division stopped by and said to the person watching as his terminal was being used, "I wish our accounting program worked as quickly as that database does, because we are having all sorts of problems." Because the software company employee knew from the Monday morning meeting that his company would be introducing a new financial service in a few weeks, he mentioned the new service and said he would have someone call. As soon as he returned to his own office, he notified his manager of the opportunity he had just heard about. A cross-selling opportunity was thus created.

A firm that encourages cross-selling does not resent the time spent nurturing existing relationships. The firm's management understands that cross-selling is an ongoing process that requires a long-term investment to achieve long-term results. It is aware that relationships are easier to maintain when you have many good contacts with an organization. Knowing a number of executives in your client's organization is an advantage because not everyone in the organization knows all its needs and because, given turnover, if you have only one contact and that contact leaves, you become an unknown quantity.

Even if you currently have no new services to offer an organization, maintaining contacts is important preparation for when you do have them to offer. If you fail to keep in touch, clients can develop new relationships that will have to be overcome. By making a few calls during the interim, you avoid losing an important entrée.

Personal Qualities

There is one thing no competitor in the world can offer your clients—you. An individual's and his company's qualities are the characteristics on which client relationships are built. A successful cross-selling effort is predicated on your ability to establish credibility and a lasting relationship with your accounts.

Clients buy more than a product or service; they buy the seller's interest and attention to their needs. They also buy the seller's reliability in delivering a quality product on time at a set price. And they buy your continued interest in seeing to it that the service or product continues to provide satisfaction.

Clients value integrity in business relationships. They are favorably impressed, for instance, when you refuse to sell them an item you do not believe is in their best interest. They appreciate it if you admit that the service you are selling may not change the course of mankind, and they respect you for not being afraid to say, "I don't know, but I'll find out"—and doing so. They will continue to buy from you if they know you will not make promises your firm will not keep, if they know you make good when there is a problem, if you describe the benefits of your company's products without denigrating your competition's, and if you refrain from attempting to oversell.

As simple as it seems, personal quality also means paying attention to such details as responding to phone calls and correspondence quickly, being prompt at meetings, and assuring that your firm has an accurate billing system.

Education and Training

Short-term relationships are built on resolving today's immediate problems—the one-shot sell. Long-term relationships have a solid foundation of understanding a client's organization and recognizing its ongoing needs. Every individual does not need to be an expert in every area, but it is important for employees to be trained to identify opportunities, to be able to discuss services conceptually, and to know when to return to the organization to call in reinforcements.

Astute cross-sellers offer *solutions* to business problems, not just services. They are consultants rather than order takers. They go out of their way to recognize problems their clients have and to anticipate future problems to determine how the services they offer may address those needs. This approach yields new opportunities to promote a greater range of problem-solving products or services.

By concentrating on your client's entire operation, rather than on a single department, you have more opportunities to deal with those higher up who have a broader responsibility for making decisions. This permits your clients to understand your entire line and each service's use and value. It also helps overcome the danger of your client saying, "I didn't know you provided that service, so I went with someone else." If you focus too early on selling a client one specific service, it becomes awkward to go back later and say, "Let me tell you something about my organization."

In cross-selling, you have to manage current relationships yet constantly seek new opportunities to exploit. Your motto should be, "When you succeed the first time, sell, sell again." After all, satisfied customers are more likely to buy additional products. For example, a computer company can sell its software to a hardware client, or a bank can offer mortgage insurance to a customer who recently has taken out a mortgage.

Remember that it is always useful to ask satisfied customers to give you referrals and introductions to others—inside or outside the company—who might need your services or to help get you on their preferred vendors list. Your clients gain the satisfaction of helping. They know that by doing so they are ensuring goodwill, and they realize that they might someday want to ask the same of you. In fact, one of the most common reasons for clients not giving referrals is that they have simply not been asked.

Incentives

No effort is effective without the proper incentive to carry it out. For cross-selling to become part of the corporate culture, it has to be encouraged both internally and externally. A company has to motivate employees to create leads for other parts of the firm and to promote the entire line each time they deal with current clients. This can be accomplished, for example, when division heads are not only compensated for the growth in their business units but for the growth in other business units as well.

There are a number of ways to reinforce a cross-selling philosophy. Among them are establishing role models by, for example, placing people with exemplary performances on pedestals. This can be accomplished by recognizing those people in front of their peers at a meeting, writing about them in the organization's internal newsletter, or placing their names on a plaque on the wall. It can also be done by creating sales-incentive programs that offer special rewards for cross-selling. This assumes that you currently have information systems that allow you to track performance;

if you cannot differentiate between effective and haphazard performance, your employees will soon realize that your reward program is meaningless.

Just as employees can be encouraged to cross-sell, clients can be motivated to purchase many products or services. One way to achieve that is to offer clients discounts for buying a variety of items or for length of time as steady customers. Furthermore, communications with long-term clients should stress the knowledge and experience built up over the years, showing that the relationship has allowed you to learn the nuances of their organization and thus given you the ability to know why a service would be especially useful to them. Such communications should also show the savings clients accrue by not having to begin new relationships.

Information Systems

Customer information is an important asset in any organization, but in many cases it is not easily accessible. It is contained in many different files and accessed by different administrative groups and business enterprises for many purposes. To support cross-selling, you must develop an integrated client database that is of high quality and easily accessible to all.

Without such timely, accurate, and manageable information, you are working in the dark. With good information, you can be confident about what you are recommending. For instance, with good information systems, you are less likely to mistake a well-established client for a first-time client. Making use of solid information prevents you from having to ask such embarrassing questions as, "In what areas are we currently doing business with you?"

Too often this is the kind of problem faced by banks where "accounting is the department that builds and drives the database." As Brad Champlin has pointed out in *Adweek's Marketing Week*, because accounting's "job isn't to market services but to manage individual accounts, banks have different data systems for each type of account. First mortgage loans are serviced on one database, deposits on another, credit cards on another, and so on."[2] This makes it hard to determine, for example, that credit card holders with low credit lines have reached the point where they are making such large payroll deposits that they clearly should be offered higher credit limits. Gary Raddon, president of the Raddon Group, says that to "identify the best cross-selling opportunities, banks must analyze the product/customer relationships and patterns."[3]

Instant, accurate information is no longer a luxury; it is vital in today's competitive business environment. Indeed, Erich Sippel, vice president of Huggins Financial Services, says that today "cross-selling really isn't about selling. It's about managing the flow of information. . . ."[4] It has become a fact of business life that you have to know all there is to know about your clients and their buying patterns, down to such details as who the clients are, where they are located, when and why they buy, what services the company has sold to them, what impact a price change or new product will have on them, and who is eligible for discounts. This kind of comprehensive information will also let you discover that a client for one of your services is buying other services you offer from another organization. You then know that something is wrong, either with your service in terms of that customer, your sales effort in that division, or some unknown stumbling block that you may be able to overcome.

Internal and External Communications

Communications are essential to a cross-selling effort. A company must keep current and inactive clients—as well as its employees—aware of the full range of capabilities it offers. This includes its latest product announcements, new service applications, and recent success stories.

The marketing campaign should be coordinated to prevent bombarding prospects with mixed, confusing messages. Materials targeted to the same audience must mesh to reinforce a common theme. If all the business units in your organization target and send information to the same audience, say, CEOs of *Fortune 500* companies, those CEOs will be confused over just what it is your company represents. Worse, if each division tries to sell the same service using different approaches, you run the risk of being perceived as disorganized—and that impression will color clients' impressions of your service. If you want to be heard clearly, your messages must be controlled so that you present outsiders with the picture of your organization that you want to convey.

Your message also has to be easily understood, address real needs, and use familiar terms. Be careful that descriptions of your new services are written in such a way that corporate executives understand the material directed to them. Although you may describe technological advances in such a way that only technicians can understand what you say and how valuable your product is, the benefits of the system must be clear to executives. If they see the strategic importance of your service, they will be more likely to ask their technical people to look into it.

Another problem is failing to maintain continuity once a service is first developed and launched. The message about its availability is too often delivered with a big initial splash, only to fade away six months later. To gain impact, reinforce the message several times using different marketing vehicles, such as capability presentations, quarterly account review meetings, newsletters, promotional literature, or VIP trips.

Implementing Cross-Selling

Senior management must present cross-selling as a high priority. For example, just as IBM named 1987 "The Year of the Customer," management would do well to announce that the coming year will be "The Year of Cross-Selling," emphasizing the fact that cross-selling will be a high priority, involving continual effort. Such an effort would emphasize that management knows that the philosophy has to permeate every part of the organization—from the highest level to the lowest, from division to division, from one functional area to another.

In order to benefit from such an undertaking, the first step should be to establish a task force either reporting to a senior executive (demonstrating management commitment) or directly involving senior executives. Even though an individual must act as a catalyst to spearhead the effort and be ultimately responsible for its success, the task force should be composed of members of various business units and functional areas (systems, training, marketing, and so forth) in order to ensure that all segments of the organization are represented and their commitment to the undertaking is secured.

The elements necessary to launching such a campaign include:

- A major firmwide educational effort defining cross-selling, promoting its benefits, and announcing the firmwide plan (endorsed by the senior executive and task force).
- Continuous reinforcement of the program and efforts to maintain its visibility throughout the year. This can be accomplished through internal/external marketing materials, meetings, internal newsletters, cross-selling bulletins, tie-ins with performance appraisals, reward programs, and promotions.
- Meetings of business unit leaders to identify areas where synergy exists between their units and others. A plan must be developed for educating and communicating this information to employees and to clients. This plan, identifying new and better ways to work together, now becomes part of the performance reviews of division heads.

Implementing such a program will accomplish a number of things. Management will not encourage local optimization at the expense of global performance. It will not tell employees not to support another member of the organization because revenue will not flow directly to their business unit. Instead, it will be making clear that what it wants done is what is good for the organization and good for the client.

When SWAT teams or specialists from different parts of the organization are assembled to address a client issue, not only is the client served better because the problem is addressed from many perspectives, but when the team is disbanded and new ones formed, the individuals who were part of the team take with them the new knowledge acquired and the new relationships formed. In the same light, rotational training programs and cross-developmental career paths contribute to a better understanding of the roles that everyone plays and thereby foster intraorganizational communications and ties.

Part of the process is ensuring that cross-selling filters down to lower levels. For example, ask all major client handlers to describe services that are now being used by the clients they deal with, and identify others that, although not tried, would address an existing need.

Networking between offices, business units, and divisions should be encouraged through regional and national meetings, consolidating newsletters and other internal communications of business units into firmwide vehicles, and introducing cross-selling modules into general training sessions. For example, an awareness of your firm's services can be incorporated into orientation programs or periodic company literacy tests—"How well do you know your organization?" Employees can be asked to take such tests for fun—with assurances they will not be graded. Each year a firmwide audiovisual presentation introducing new services and reinforcing old ones can be distributed. Finally, you can distribute product sheets describing each service (in language that is easily understood), explaining how to identify (for the layperson) opportunities for the service based on clients' problems, pointing out who in the organization has expertise in various areas, and listing the major contacts for information.

You can also promote new ideas and new thinking by circulating success stories and case studies highlighting what has worked in the past. For example, present a success story about three people from three different business units who collectively made a presentation to a potential client. Also relate stories about the tactics used by organizations that successfully cross-sell. One such example is CIGNA, which used a number of different strategies to ensure that cross-selling became an integral part of its corporate structure. CIGNA saw to it that:

- Local directories were published so that field people could contact their counterparts in other areas of the company.
- The company established a Cross-Selling Hotline where individuals could phone in their cross-selling ideas.
- Separate divisions jointly organized local trade fairs.
- Over $2 million was pumped into a new integrated customer database that could facilitate the tracking of cross-divisional sales.[5]

Conclusion

Think about what cross-selling could do for your organization. Remember the bank teller and assistant manager? Both would have known about the life insurance program in an organization in which an everybody sells philosophy was reinforced. In other words, that customer might have ended up buying her insurance from the bank if its employees had been properly trained to cross-sell, if the message about the insurance program had been reinforced through communications, if they had had access to information about the whole customer from the beginning, and if they were made aware that efforts to promote sales of insurance to customers would win them praise and even rewards.

Cross-selling offers practically limitless opportunities. But cross-selling does not just happen. All the elements are important, and all work together like the sections of a symphony orchestra. But above all, successful cross-selling requires the proper mind-set, with every individual in the organization on the alert for promising opportunities.

As long as everyone understands what cross-selling takes, that it is a constant, it will pay off. Your company can multiply its income and its profits better when it explores new opportunities with current clients instead of scrambling constantly for new ones. It's simple arithmetic.

13

Playing Politics: Vote No

Politicians are elected to serve their constituencies; those who vote for them do so because they believe that the candidates they are voting for will improve conditions in the country. In the same way, executives are chosen to lead firms because stakeholders believe that they will make the firms more efficient and more profitable, thereby improving their long-term competitive position.

Unfortunately, politics in both the political and business realm all too often is synonymous with *playing politics,* which can be deadly. Politicians are kept from fulfilling their constituents' mandates by the demands of special interests, whose thousands of lobbyists ply their trade from their permanent offices in Washington, D.C. Executives are kept from fulfilling their stakeholders' goals by employees who spend their time "lobbying" for personal goals rather than corporate goals. All this is part of the game of politics.

The terms associated with playing politics make the nature of the disease clear—backstabbing, maneuvering, doing an end-run, infighting, shifting the blame, covering your behind, building a case, railroading a decision, developing strategies against the opposition, fighting the bureaucracy, defending your turf, building a power base, stealing the credit, defending your interests.

Playing politics is a form of noncooperation in an organization that is similar to the war that goes on in the body when parts of a cell fight one another. In the body the result is a cancer—leukemia—that kills without radical treatment; in business the treatment must be just as radical once the line between being politically astute and playing games has been blurred.

The Root of the Problem

You must understand the reasons for your employees' preoccupation with playing politics if you want to try to stop them from doing it. Often playing politics becomes the principal occupation of employees when an organization does not have a clear mission, when it lacks leaders who define its goals clearly, when people do not understand their proper roles, and when the organization has a vague performance measurement and reward system. At such times, the members of an organization tend to take things into their own hands. The situation is analogous to two people trying to move a table by pulling it in opposite directions. When a firm operates in this way, individuals end up striving to attain their personal goals even if it means working at cross-purposes with other members of the organization.

In these situations, intense competition builds within the organization for limited resources, money, prestige, power, and position. As a result of the effort spent on these battles, communication is hindered, intergroup hostility paralyzes performance, and subcultures emerge. There is little coordination between players in the organization, and activities that are critical to the firm's functioning do not get done. Playing politics becomes the firm's main enterprise, and the result is poor performance.

In such a climate, internal politics—who said what to whom, who is gaining power, and who gets credit, who blame—overshadows clients' needs, inroads by the competition, or overall organizational performance. The results are like a snowball that picks up speed as it rolls down a hill. Things go from bad to worse: People choose the most politically astute solution rather than the best solution. The "show" internal meetings become more important than a meeting's contents; promotions are earned through political savvy rather than performance; and rumor becomes the most common form of communication.

Employees begin to look over their shoulders before they take any action; they keep their ideas and experiences close to their vests in the hope of becoming irreplaceable; they opt for safe solutions. Creative and innovative employees find their morale slipping and leave. People say, "Why should I fight for the right cause when it isn't appreciated anyway?" or "I don't care if I'm doing the right thing or just keeping busy because I don't plan to be here tomorrow." Finally, turnover of the best employees makes it more difficult for a firm to attract talented people because over time it develops a poor reputation.

All the while, senior management wonders why the firm isn't competitive, why productivity gains haven't been achieved, why quality is lacking, why the organization isn't innovative, why profitability targets are missed, why market share is lost, why employee turnover is high, why two people seem to be needed to do a job that used to be done by one, why burnout occurs, and why, when it examines the situation more carefully, people excel at their outside activities but are apathetic and mediocre at work. What they need to do is ask what makes some groups act in unison while others embrace diversion. Why do some people behave constructively while others behave destructively? And why do some groups have a commitment to carry out responsibilities while others are apathetic?

Tomorrow's Leader

"One of the key problems facing many modern organizations," according to Warren Bennis and Burt Nanus, "is that they are underled and overmanaged. Their top people do not pay enough attention to doing the right thing, while they pay too much attention to doing things right."[1]

Good organizations place a high value on doing what is necessary to make the firm prosper over the long term, including making investments in areas that do not provide immediate returns. In good organizations members of one department will give up good people to another for the good of the firm, executives don't refuse to train people because "training takes people away from their jobs, so why do it?" and people do not hire bodies to fill vacancies, they search for the right people for positions. It means promoting and reinforcing the beliefs and values on which the organization is based, and setting high ethical standards for the firm. In *A Business and Its Beliefs,* Thomas Watson, Jr., an original founder of IBM, said, "Beliefs must always come before policies, practices, and goals. The latter must always be altered if they are seen to violate fundamental beliefs. The only sacred cow in an organization should be its basic philosophy of doing business."[2]

Tomorrow's leaders must do more than manage numbers and be caretakers of the day-to-day business, pressuring employees for immediate results even at the expense of tomorrow. Tomorrow's leaders must be able to articulate a vision, enlist support and involvement for a common cause, and cement bonds between people—pulling rather than pushing toward a goal.

Roger Smith, CEO of General Motors, in discussing what happened when he first assumed command at GM, notes:

> I sure wish I'd done a better job of communicating with GM people. I'd do that differently a second time around and make sure that they understood and shared my vision for the company. Then they would have known why I was tearing the place up, taking out whole divisions, changing our whole production structure. If people understand the *why,* they'll work at it. Like I say, I never got all this across. There we were, charging up the hill right on schedule, and I looked behind me and saw that many people were still at the bottom, trying to decide whether to come along. I'm talking about hourly workers, middle management, even some top managers. It seemed like a lot of them had gotten off the train.[3]

A leader's prime responsibility is to provide direction and make clear what that direction is. The staff of an organization is not unlike any other group of people—afraid of the unknown and in need of direction. This fear is compounded by the recent activity of takeovers, mergers, downsizing, and divestitures occurring at many companies. Lawrence Schein, senior research associate at the Conference Board, says that "mergers and acquisitions present tremendous opportunities for organizational conflict and confusion, particularly when two very diverse corporate cultures are forced to adapt to each other."[4]

Playing politics can become a way of life in such situations. The worst problems that develop center on the "us" and "them" mentality that emerges in these difficult, unsettling situations. In an analysis of the problems caused by the deregulation of AT&T in the *Wall Street Journal,* a manager for one of the Bell operating companies said that "the tension between insiders and outsiders is so suffocating that he is having nightmares about it. In one dream, he is drowning while his co-workers stand on shore, ignoring him."[5] In the same article, another new employee said, "Our biggest opposition doesn't come from the competition. It comes from people within the company."

An organization's executives must accept responsibility for countering this kind of mentality. They must let employees know where they stand and let them know that they will not tolerate this kind of behavior. They must, as early as possible, make it clear that there will be changes, but that there will also be opportunities and that employees will be dealt with fairly. After all, most employees want leaders who are reliable and consistent. Knowing what the boss thinks in advance causes people to perform as expected. Inconsistent behavior—waffling—makes people anxious because they cannot manage their expectations. Therefore, management should always make sure that its behavior is consistent with its stated goals. By doing so, managers become positive role models whose behavior is emulated.

The primary roles of executives should include motivating employees, helping them grow and develop personally and professionally, and inspiring them to achieve their maximum potential. One important challenge created by rapidly changing technology is finding a way to help people overcome their belief that such changes are threatening. Leaders can do that by encouraging and aiding employees to grow and learn through education and training. If they fail to do so, walls will be built between those who understand and can apply technology and those who cannot.

In addition, tomorrow's leaders should demand and participate in a never-ending search for the right people, and then they must ensure that those people are assimilated into the organization quickly and effectively. They must create a climate of teamwork, caring, and support for their fellow workers, encouraging innovative ideas and new ways of thinking. Most of all, they must encourage leadership at all levels in an organization and assure employees that they have important roles to play in moving the organization forward.

For example, Andrew Grove, a founder and president of Intel

Corporation, explains that in his company, which must adapt constantly to enormous technological changes, it is critical that the executives and those knowledgeable about technology communicate frequently and easily. He says that as a result, junior members of the organization are often asked "to participate jointly in decision-making meetings with senior management." But, he warns,

> This only works if everyone at the meeting voices opinions and beliefs as *equals,* forgetting or ignoring status differentials. And it is much easier to achieve this if the organization doesn't separate its senior and junior people with limousines, plush offices, and private dining rooms. Status symbols [in an organization like Intel] do not promote the flow of ideas, facts, and points of view.

Grove believes that this style of operating is necessary for high-tech industries and may prove advantageous in other kinds of businesses: "Perhaps if all of American industry broke down the walls between knowledge and power, we would begin to regain our lead in the more highly competitive world market in which we all have to live and operate."[6]

This is just one example of the ways in which leadership can work to bring its employees together and create an environment in which playing politics is unnecessary. If senior management takes this kind of care to communicate with employees and show them how valuable their contributions are, employees will know where they stand and what kind of effort is expected of them. Then all they have to do is perform.

Cooperating Versus Competing

Putting an end to playing politics requires a concerted effort throughout an organization. Sun Tsu's *The Art of War* says, "In war, the general receives his command from the sovereign. Having collected an army and concentrated his forces, he must blend and harmonize the different elements . . . [he will] not succeed unless [his] men have tenacity and unity of purpose, and, above all, a spirit of sympathetic cooperation." Yet in a recent study conducted by Robert Lefton and V. R. Buzzotta of 26 companies

(20 among the *Fortune 500*), the members acknowledged that less than 40 percent of their interaction could be called teamwork.[7]

In establishing the mission, goals, objectives, and strategies for an organization, discussion is important because it serves as a team-building exercise and places people on a common wavelength. Even if management has already decided on its vision and strategy, participation by those at lower levels is important. When employees are told what to do rather than having their support enlisted, they are more likely to go through the motions. Management finds itself interpreting blank stares that mean "I don't care" or "I don't understand" as "Yes, I agree" or "Of course, I'll do it."

Management often provides less information to its employees than it realizes. An *Industry Week* survey revealed that even though "almost 60% (57.9) of top management respondents believe they are telling employees more, . . . only half as many (30%) of the non-management respondents feel that way. In fact, 35% of the non-management replies indicated they are being told less." Perhaps more important, when "asked what the company was sharing with employees, information about sales, products, and benefits was checked more often than information concerning company policies and strategy, competitors, or profits."[8]

Remember that it is not enough for some privileged group to know the game plan. All employees must feel part of it and believe they are playing an integral role in achieving the organization's goals. And the roles that employees are expected to play must be clearly defined. It is up to the firm's leadership to find ways to employ its staff's unique talents so that they contribute to the overall team's success. The rationale for doing a specific task should be explained to all those whose collaboration will be needed to achieve its success. Clearly defining responsibility will help prevent personality clashes that result in no one accepting it and the buck being passed like a hot potato or in many people feeling responsible and crowded out.

Employees must also learn to put themselves in other people's shoes so that they can understand their needs, values, cultures, and viewpoints. Differences among countries, regions, and departments in an organization, or in levels in one, can lead to misunderstandings and miscommunication. These differences also lead to problems when new employees are brought into an organization.

The result of ignoring these problems is all too often a "we" versus "they" mentality that must be corrected. Such a situation had developed at U.S. West, when a group of new employees were brought into the organization. At a retreat, U.S. West's chairman Jack MacAllister confronted his executives with the problem headlong. "Holding up a sign that read 'Outsiders,' he paraded in front of two seated executives who had recently joined the company. People in the audience chuckled knowingly. Then the chairman ripped up the card. 'Once they're hired by this company, they're no longer outsiders.' "[9]

In addition to learning to accept such changes, those working for an organization must be taught not only how they can best perform their jobs but what others have to do to perform theirs so that they are sympathetic in their demands on others. Employees should meet one another under proper conditions rather than first meeting colleagues under tight time pressures and impossible deadlines. With the right kind of training and direction, groups will be able to negotiate decisions in a clear and open environment that will foster trust, creativity, growth, and teamwork.

Communication: A Means to an End

"Communication creates meaning for people . . . getting the message across unequivocally at every level is an absolute key and . . . separates the managers from the leaders," according to Warren Bennis and Burt Nanus.[10]

Communication is the vehicle by which leaders focus and direct their employees. In managing internal communications, often a great deal of time is lost nit-picking words rather than ensuring that all activities, no matter how trivial they may seem, are consistent in meaning and bring about desired behavior. More, managers must recognize that two kinds of communications systems are at work, the formal and informal (sometimes called the grapevine). If these two systems seem to provide different messages, employees spend more time trying to ferret out hidden meanings in all the communications that cross their desks than in working.

What makes matters worse is that frequently "some 80 percent of the original message is lost in its transmission pattern from top management to the implementation level. A growing organization experiencing normal communication problems may be hard-pressed to carry out its functional ideas with a minimum of misunderstanding."[11] Informal channels of communication can help alleviate the problem if they are carefully managed.

An example of the proper use of informal communications took place at a Du Pont plant that was reorganizing to modernize its production facilities. Bob Wooten, a professor of business administration at Lamar University, explains:

> Concerned about possible misunderstanding and morale deterioration among the involved employees, the plant's managers instituted a program promoting an informal system of communication encouraging questions, feedback, and personal discussions between management and employees. The program lasted for several months and proved to be a major step toward providing employees with an appreciation of organizational problems.[12]

Wooten believes that effective communication requires a mix of formal and informal communications; the personal contact involved in an informal channel reinforces and clarifies communications coming down from the highest executive levels.

Successful communication is part of the answer to the problem raised by Thomas Watson, Jr., when he was asked how an organization keeps employees pulling together, despite diversity in interests. How do you shorten the distance between levels in an organization and maintain the small company attitudes that were instrumental to IBM's success? "From 1946 through 1962 IBM's worldwide population increased by more than 100,000 people. We had to face the problem of how to implant and keep alive in these people a real feeling for the traditions and beliefs of the business."[13] This problem is the same one facing countless other growing organizations.

IBM responded by instituting an employee question-and-answer program that enhanced upward communication, by starting a newsletter providing managers with the *why* behind policies, by instituting informal family dinners to maintain a small company attitude, and by sending congratulatory letters on promotions and jobs well-done to show that someone cared.

A failure to communicate company values and beliefs makes them lose meaning over time. Messages need constant reinforcement. Leaders set the tone in many different ways—through the individuals they surround themselves with; how they set their priorities; by the consistency of their actions and their words; and by the ways in which they promote people and the ways in which they introduce new people to the organization. They set the tone by everything from bulletin boards to company T-shirts; meeting formats to size and location of offices; office hours to access to executives; holiday parties to retirement dinners; internal newsletters to dress codes. What is critical is that the signals be sent through many mediums and be consistent in meaning.

Sending and maintaining positive messages is half the job of communicating well enough to avoid an atmosphere in which playing politics becomes the modus vivendi. The other half is getting people to listen. Why is so much emphasis placed on transmitting information—speaking and writing—and so little on receiving it? How many errors occur because directions are misunderstood? How many arguments occur because motives are misinterpreted? How much information is lost as people shuffle papers, ask irrelevant questions, or talk on the phone in the middle of another conversation?

These are all barriers to communication. In order to improve communication in an organization managers should first ask:

1. Is English or Acronym our first language? (People must be encouraged to communicate rather than impress. New employees must not be automatically locked out of the net by a language barrier.)

2. How well do we handle meetings? Are meeting agendas and objectives made clear through memoranda distributed beforehand? Is everyone encouraged to contribute, or do attendees come to hear the boss speak? Do the meetings stay on track or turn into griping sessions? When groups meet on a regular basis, is attendance mandatory, ensuring that members of the same group remain on the same wavelength?

3. How much time is spent improving the process—that is, the interaction between attendees—rather than the content of meetings? Are people reprimanded for their comments and made to fear a backlash for presenting different opinions? Do people deal well enough with one another that defensive behavior is unusual? Is two-way dialogue the norm, or is grandstanding more common? Is courtesy usual in dealing with one another?

4. When new ideas surface, are they objectively discussed and built upon, or do people gain pleasure from shooting them down and discarding them?

5. Do people try to make decisions with inaccurate and incomplete information, or are they encouraged to work with other members of the organization to arrive at an optimum solution?

6. Does communication flow one way (downward), or do you strive through human relations and management practices, audits, surveys, and interviews to get candid feedback from employees?

7. Is communication managed or just allowed to happen? Unless communication is encouraged and creative and innovative ideas are allowed to flourish, an organization will falter.

Rewards and Recognition

John Kotter of Harvard University has said, "Perhaps the most common answer regarding what makes the work environment fun is lack of politics."[14] One certain way to avoid having people play politics as a way of work is to be sure that good work is recognized and rewarded clearly and quickly. The failure to provide employees with motivation can cause serious problems, as is evident from this story of a General Motors employee, which was reported in a study of corporations. The employee wrote in a letter to a friend, "Knowing that I never had a chance to be anything within the company, the next obvious move was for me to become active in the local union. . . . I now had a cause . . . to screw the sons of bitches in management that had been too good to recognize me as another human being." After realizing

that General Motors was being destroyed by this kind of thinking, the employee changed his mind. He said, "We have to truly
change if we are to survive. We have to care about the consumer
. . . the stockholders . . . the people we represent. But most
important, management people and workers have to care about
each other."[15]

Rewards must be consistent with and reinforce the goals of an
organization. They must be clearly understood, flexible enough
to change as a business's strategy changes, and be directly tied to
performance. After all, performance is measurable; good managers can easily differentiate between high and low performers.
Results are important, not time spent on the job. Although efforts
should be praised, rewards should be linked to performance, not
intent.

Many companies have realized the benefits of a policy of publicly rewarding workers who perform well. The *Wall Street Journal*
reports that awards such as Colgate-Palmolive's "You Can Make
a Difference Award," which is given as part of a weeklong tribute
to notable employees along with $3,500 in stock, is all part of an
"accelerating corporate trend to honor output, service, or longevity with public mention and maybe some gifts or cash."[16]

Rewarding people for working well with others, as well as
rewarding those who accomplish individual goals that contribute
to the group effort, sets a norm. It allows management to emphasize the importance it places on its primary agenda by showing
its disdain for internal politics. Management must be evaluated
for its ability to motivate staff, foster teamwork, and achieve
long-term goals. Promotions should be used to reward apolitical
attitudes that put the organization's needs ahead of personal
goals—the ability to be a good team player.

Conclusion

Corporate leaders must spend their time guiding or influencing
policy. They must lead their firms out of the dead end of political gamesmanship into a future focused on a corporate ethic of
achievement. To do so, they must concentrate on the people
who do the work that fills their customers' needs and on seeing

to it that the corporate culture is an open one. They must encourage leadership to keep lines of communication open, construct a corporate environment in which everyone feels a part of the team, and reward performance. That will bring an end to the evils caused by playing politics, a game in which there are no winners.

14

Success: A Lifetime Stroll on a Tightrope

Our exploration of the road to successful marketing began with an examination of the problems created when individuals decide to wing it. We then went on to examine the importance of properly executing business strategies to the success of the individual as well as the firm. Now it is time for self-examination, exploring your own makeup to determine whether you have the characteristics that will help you succeed and finding ways to overcome any negative traits you may have.

Years of observing successful marketers and successful business leaders have brought me some understanding of the attributes necessary to achieve success. In analyzing what I had learned through observation, I discovered that someone else was doing the same thing; as a result, this chapter is a collaboration with Ed Rosen, the founder of two organizations that, respectively, exceeded $40 million and $100 million in revenues before he sold them and became a consultant. What we learned as we worked together was that the qualities of successful entrepreneurs and successful marketers are very similar; indeed, further study made it clear that those who achieve any kind of success tend to have certain definable traits.

Basically, the characteristics of the successful individual can be divided into two categories: The first, broadly stated, includes personal endowments and overall mind-set—that is, who you are and your approaches to living; the second includes a very specific set of people and business skills that a successful person develops and nurtures. The analyses of the different characteristics that follow, along with the scales provided, will help you decide where you fall on the continuum—the tightrope connecting the various possibilities associated with those characteristics—and how you can achieve the kind of balance on the tightrope that will enable you to win at marketing.

Who Are You?

What are your personal endowments? How have your upbringing and education affected you? What assumptions and beliefs guide you? The answers to these questions will tell you who you are and what you can do to improve your chances for success. You should be better able to answer such questions as, do you need to learn more about yourself? What things about yourself must change if you are to grow?

Assessing Your Personal Endowments

Strong Body	Strong Mind

You are born with genes that to some extent determine what you will be able to do; your genes have some control over your future. If you are a man five feet tall, you stand little chance of making it to the National Football League, but if you want to excel in sports, everything from gymnastics to weightlifting to being the rider of the Triple Crown winner is open to you. What it requires is determination and hard work.

No matter what kind of physical endowments you were born with, make the most of them. Maintaining good **health** is critical to your success in every aspect of your life; you need stamina for all the contests you enter. And the better you feel about yourself, the better your outlook on life. Exercise is a major road to gaining that feeling of strength. It is also a good way to reduce stress and improve emotional stability.

Intelligence	Utilization

The other major determinant of your success that is, to some extent, determined for you is intelligence. Having a good memory or a high IQ is no assurance of success. You must use your innate intelligence, training your mind as well as your body. Knowledge may be easier or harder to acquire given your particular inborn capacity; what determines your success is how well you **apply your mental abilities**.

Work Life	Personal Life

Once you have left home and school and set out on your own, you must shape your personal life in such a way that it becomes an asset. Your **personal life** must provide enough satisfaction and escape to enable you to give your all when you are at work. And you must be careful not to let the problems in one area destroy the rewards and pleasure you get from the other. Being hard-working is important, but being a workaholic, allowing work to become your whole life, may cause problems at home, which then may adversely affect your ability to perform well.

Belief Structures

Clear	Cloudy

Our early years help instill in us **ethical values** that are refined through experience. Knowing right from wrong is easy when the case is clear-cut: Murder is wrong. But sometimes the lines are not as clear. Stealing is wrong, but how many of us think we are stealing when we put a pen in our pocket at work and bring it home? The lines blur even more if you take the pen home because you want to use it to finish the project you were working on that day, but then you do not bring it back.

At times you feel uncomfortable because something disturbs your ethical values. For example, if someone asks you to work on a project and you find yourself uneasy every time you think about it, take a closer look. If there is something about the project that disturbs your sense of ethics, figure out what it is, explain the problem to those in charge, and refuse to continue until the problem is solved to your satisfaction.

Expediency	Loyalty

One of the values you develop early is **loyalty.** Almost everyone grows up with a sense of loyalty to family and country. That is then extended, as your horizons expand, to friends and eventually to institutions and organizations you become part of. If you allow yourself to be loyal only when it is convenient, to switch allegiances as it suits your needs, you only damage yourself. You will quickly begin to assume that everyone else does the same thing and resist commitment; in the end, you distrust others and do not feel very good about yourself.

Say	Do

Maintaining **integrity** (always doing what you say you are going to do) is another basic value that makes you what you are. Most people will trust someone to deliver on a promise the first few times. If the person lets them down, they no longer believe that the person will follow through on future commitments. If you gain that kind of reputation, it will destroy relationships on every level, costing you the respect of friends and co-workers and eventually self-esteem.

Acquired Characteristics

Effort	Perseverance

Strength of mind is another quality that seems innate. Some people try something once, and having made the effort and failed, move on to try something else. Successful people tend to react to their initial failure by trying again. "If at first you don't succeed, try, try again" seems to be something that comes naturally to them. But it is a quality that can be learned.

Your Own	Others

The ability and wisdom to **learn from mistakes** are traits you develop early in life. You must learn both from your own mistakes, which takes the ability to admit that you were wrong in the first place, and from the mistakes of others, which means that you don't have to repeat every mistake yourself. But be careful not to assume that what goes wrong for someone else will go wrong for you; assess the differences in what you bring to an endeavor. For example, you should not decide that, because three restaurants that opened in a given neighborhood failed, yours will also. Investigate who opened them, what price range they were appealing to, the kind of food they served, what kind of financial backing they had, and what went wrong. Knowing what mistakes they made might allow you to succeed.

Bare Minimum	Furthest Stretch

Discovering a process for setting **personal goals** is part of your personal growth. Successful people have learned to set optimistic but realistic goals, aspiring to things that will make them stretch to their fullest potential. Once you achieve a little more than you hoped to, it becomes easier to raise your goals. If you set your sights too low, you can fool yourself into believing you have done well, but only for a short time.

Striving for Perfection	Working on What Counts

Although it is good to be the best you can be, sometimes the amount of energy and effort required to reach perfection—that last 5 percent—may not be the optimum way to use your time. Weigh the value of that last 5 percent against the opportunity costs of not doing something else: In other words, **set priorities.**

Doing What You Enjoy	Doing What Must Be Done

You must learn how to **take the good with the bad.** Every activity cannot be enjoyable. Those who succeed have learned to work through unpleasant activities by looking ahead to what is next. Those who are unsuccessful spend as much time protesting as it would take to do the job.

Approaches to Living

Your outlook on life will determine how you will handle responsibilities and manage your day-to-day activities. Your basic inborn qualities limit you only if you allow them to. Your job is to move yourself toward equilibrium, toward the most effective point on the continuum.

Always Learning

Dedication	Ability

No matter how hard you work, you cannot succeed unless you also have the necessary **skills** to achieve your goals. Take that night course; attend that seminar; read that book; go for that extra degree.

Conformance	Finding a Better Way

When you are on top, it is hard to think about changing. But reexamination must become a habit. Avoid complacency and make **continuous improvement** your goal. Keep in mind the differences between change that is necessary, change for improvement, and change for the sake of change.

Stop to Enjoy Successes	Full Steam Ahead

You must learn to maintain a balance between going all out in pursuit of your goals, never pausing to enjoy what you have achieved, and reaching a point where you're so far ahead you decide to stop working so hard. If you come to a full stop, it is very hard to regain **momentum** if it becomes necessary. Tom Seaver once said that the worst thing a pitcher could do is relax when his team had a big lead; if the other team ever caught up, it would be much more difficult to step on the accelerator again.

Motion	Movement

Some people try to impress others by how hard they work, how many hours they have spent on something, or how many tasks they have completed. But were the activities productive? Was the time invested wisely? Some people are so convinced that motion is what counts that they endlessly run in circles, without stopping to plan how to get from point A to point B. You cannot **attain your goals** without planning or purpose.

Alternate Opportunities	Concentration of Efforts

Most of the decisions you make require sorting through any number of alternatives to arrive at the best options. Once you determine the best path for your organization to follow, make certain you do not divert your attention to other matters, even if they seem inviting. **Focus** all your resources on your priorities.

Knowing Yourself and the World Around You

Yourself	Others

Remember that people admire those who demand the same of themselves that they demand from others. If you want to succeed and motivate others, you must be a **role model** for those around you.

Rewards	Responsibilities

You should balance your expectations between your responsibilities and the rewards you will receive. The first step is **understanding the commitments** you have made and the rewards you are likely to achieve for meeting them. Later, when you are given more responsibilities and handle them well, you should receive greater rewards.

Yourself	Organization

To succeed, you must avoid focusing on "what's in it for me." If you adopt a philosophy of hard work, continued learning, adding value, and working in the best interests of the organization, you will discover that it is a **quid pro quo** world.

How Things Are	How They Should Be

Learn early to strike a balance between the real and the ideal. In today's competitive environment, there is so much pressure on performance that we lose sight of **reality.** In business, a failure to find balance on this continuum results in, for example, enormous amounts of time and energy spent manipulating statistics to prove goals were met instead of correcting the problem that caused the shortfall.

Immediate Gratification	Patience

Learn early that it is never wise to live only for the moment. To succeed, you should try to adopt the **longest-term perspective** you can. Learn to avoid quick job hops for better pay or overselling a client to win an incentive award. Life is a marathon, not a sprint, and that means setting the best pace—giving up the short-term lead to position yourself to win the race.

Risk	Reward

Some people are willing to leave the **comfort zone,** accepting the risk, for example, of leaving the security of a job to start their own business. They know that the risks are high, but they believe the rewards are worth it. Those who follow in the footsteps of the ground breakers must remember that the first one to start a new enterprise is likely to receive the greatest rewards, with later entrants in the field running to catch up before they can hope to get ahead. Those heading traditional organizations must also always keep an eye on new developments that might help their company grab a leading share, determining if the risks of, say, buying a million-dollar computer system are worth the possible rewards.

People Skills

The two categories we have just examined will help you see how you react to situations and deal with people. In business, the ease with which you adjust to new situations and the way in which you are perceived both make a difference. The better you are with people, the more likely you are to succeed: Reach out to others and motivate them to work with you to find ways of achieving success for themselves, for you, and for your organization.

Popularity	Doing the Right Thing

Because everyone enjoys being admired by those who know them, it is always hardest to make decisions that will be unpopular, at least at the moment. **Leadership** is that quality that enables you to have the strength to do what is right for the greatest good, even if it momentarily makes those adversely affected by your decision unhappy with you.

Highs	Lows

During the course of your career, you will experience both good times and bad. The key is to keep a level head when things are going well and to avoid falling into a depression when they are not. You must learn how to deal with the best and the worst in such a way that they do not adversely affect your business life. You must also keep in mind that the **morale** of those you work with can be affected by yours.

Motivating Yourself	Motivating Others

If you hope to **climb the organizational ladder,** remember that although at the outset you are measured by your personal productivity, as you rise in the organization, emphasis shifts to your ability to motivate others. You must move across the continuum carefully, maintaining the right balance at all times.

Knowing What Needs Doing	Motivating Others To Do It

It is one thing to know what actions should be taken to implement a plan; it is another to be able to execute the plan. **Execution** requires motivating others to work with you, pulling your team together by empowering them. Poor managers tend to push people to act by inspiring fear.

Abdicating Responsibility	Delegating Responsibility

If you have the ability and training to be a **good manager,** you have learned that merely assigning responsibility to a team is not enough; you must practice careful oversight. Learn how to set up structures in which those you give responsibilities to report back to you periodically. Remember that you are the person who will be held accountable for the results.

Note Weakness	Praise Strength

It is always easier to identify a person's weakness than to recognize a person's strengths. The result is that all too often strengths are taken for granted. If you are **perceptive about people,** you can find ways to praise an employee's strengths publicly, making those qualities something the individual's peers emulate.

Observing	Praising

It is not enough to see the good things in people; let them know you appreciate what they are doing. See to it that **recognition** and rewards are the result of your perception.

Victory at All Costs	Compromise

Learning to **choose your battles** instead of fighting every one on every front is critical. Success comes to those who select the battles they want to wage, know what is worth fighting for, and compromise on those where the odds of winning are too small to warrant the expense of the battle.

Maintaining Friendships	Making Acquaintances

Sometimes people rising to the top of the corporate ladder forget the people who helped them get there. They believe that they have outgrown their old buddies or that they do not need them any more. If you do not maintain **alliances** forged throughout your career, you will find it rather lonely at the top.

Business Skills

The second set of skills that help determine how you fare in business are those you develop through experience in the business world. They are a combination of the information you have acquired through schooling and on-the-job learning with your inherent analytic skills and ability to deal with people. These skills come together to make you someone who can make things happen.

Start-up Skills

Superiors	Subordinates

Some individuals spend their whole lives trying to impress their superiors. They do all the right things for those above them: They keep them informed, respect their wishes, make their every request a priority. They spend little time **making an impression** on those they work with and those who work for them. Somewhere along the line, they have missed the point. You cannot do it all by yourself. If you have not won the respect of those at your level and below, you will have a much more difficult time achieving success. No one will want to go that extra step for you.

Persistence	Following Orders

Drive is a critical component of the successful individual. After all, it normally requires tremendous persistence to spearhead new ideas in an organization or set up a new business. What is necessary to make drive work for you is the experience to temper the push. Know how far you can go before you damage your cause, your career, and your chance of being effective in the future. At some point, you must be willing to lay down the sword, be a team player, and go along with someone else's viewpoint—and you must be able to do it gracefully.

Speaking	Listening

A good part of your life has been spent learning how to communicate orally and in writing. No matter how effective you have been in the past, if you sharpen your listening skills, you will garner more respect. Moreover, you must hear the needs and desires of others if you are to motivate them. Once you have learned to listen, your written and oral **communication skills** can take you even further.

Personalities	Issues

Successful managers create an environment that encourages free and open discussions. In any environment that fosters this kind of dialogue, **debate** should always focus on issues, never on the personalities involved.

Getting Things Done

Identifying Problems	Recommending Solutions

Identifying the problem areas within an organization is only half the job. In fact, if you are perceived as too quick to point out problems and complain without ever recommending solutions, you develop a reputation for being unproductive. It is a little like looking at someone lying on the sidewalk, knowing that the individual needs medical attention, then walking away, assuming that someone else will call for help. You must learn the art of **problem resolution** to be effective in any area of your life.

Critique	Create

It is usually easy to find fault with recommendations that people make to resolve particular problems. Before you gain a reputation as someone who always shoots down other people's **ideas,** be sure to have recommendations of your own to present.

Theory	Commercialization

Developing theories and investigating them are important, but so is the eventual product that results from **research.** The business challenge is to find a way to commercialize pure research and theoretical ideas. (Of course, scientific and medical research are different. And so is the kind of research sponsored by other institutions set up for pure research.)

Qualify	Quantify

We all admire people who can find creative solutions to difficult problems. The real test is not coming up with the idea, but in being able to **quantify the idea.** Will it work? Can it be implemented?

React	Anticipate

It is never enough to react to problems as they develop. The good manager is a **planner** who not only anticipates problems but finds ways to deal with them before they occur.

Format	Content

Learn to avoid evaluating a plan by the way it is packaged. Format cannot make up for weaknesses in the strategies the **plan** is based on.

Planning	Implementation

People who are successful both develop plans and see to it that they are properly implemented. Once it was possible to succeed in business by having special groups for planning and others for implementing. The business world has changed so much that those who can **balance those skills** will go furthest.

Getting There

You started reading this book because you are one of those people who aims to get to the top. You hope to achieve a solid success in the world of business as quickly as you can and are willing to work to get what you want. You are searching for all the right tools. Let me ask you a question before showing you how to apply what you have just learned about constantly reevaluating yourself. What happens when you get there? That is, have you thought about how to manage your success?

Rational Decision Making	Overconfidence

Sometimes people develop a belief in their own infallibility, a sense of omnipotence, that makes them abandon the rules that got them to the top. They get sloppy, ignore people, look only to their own interests. If you do not **manage your success,** continuing to base your decisions on sound information and advice, you may end up losing everything you've worked so hard to achieve.

The idea of the continuum is to provide a useful tool for establishing your position, thereby helping you maintain your balance on the tightrope to success. Obviously, endless aspects of business life require walking a fine line. When you come to something that troubles you, look at it from as many sides as possible. Decide what your boundaries are, and create your own continuum.

For example, if you have an artist in your advertising agency who always produces wonderful but extremely expensive and elaborate designs, it may cost you clients. They may accept the designs because they are so good, but after a while they will discover that they are spending far more than is necessary to get the job done. Why should they use four-color brochures when two-color brochures always brought in the same amount of business? Because they cannot pinpoint the problem, they simply decide your firm is too expensive.

When confronted with a problem, you should set up a continuum; in the case just described, it would look something like this:

Too Low	**Too High**

Providing low **quality service** is obviously a problem for any organization, but there is also a risk in providing service that is too high—more than the client needs. It is cost-ineffective.

Use this concept to analyze all of the challenges that come your way. Instead of taking things for granted and living your life by sheer momentum, always ask yourself whether you are centered properly on the continuum.

Notes

Chapter 2

1. Gerhard Gschwandtner and Laura B. Gschwandtner, *Supersellers* (New York: Amacom, 1986).

2. "Brainstorming," in *Boardroom Reports,* May 1, 1989, p. 15.

Chapter 3

1. Robert Denney, "Marketing Lawyers," *Wall Street Journal,* February 26, 1987, p. B1.

2. Sumner Myers and Eldon E. Sweezy, "Why Innovations Fail," *Technology Review,* March–April 1978, p. 39.

3. Roger von Oech, *A Kick in the Seat of the Pants* (New York: Harper & Row, 1986), p. 25.

4. Patricia Bellew Gray, "Profile in Failure: One Man's Painful Crash," *Wall Street Journal,* December 15, 1986, p. 30.

5. Alecia Swasy, "Slow and Steady," *Wall Street Journal,* September 21, 1989, p. A12.

6. Tom Peters, *Thriving on Chaos* (New York: Alfred A. Knopf, 1987), p. 265.

7. Warren Bennis and Burt Nanus, *Leaders: The Strategies for Taking Charge* (New York: Harper & Row, 1985), p. 39.

8. Von Oech, p. 109.

9. Stratford P. Sherman, "The Mind of Jack Welch," *Fortune,* March 27, 1989, p. 40.

10. Sherman, p. 50.

11. William E. Peacock, *Corporate Combat* (New York: The Berkley Publishing Group, 1984), p. 188.

12. This section draws on Philip Koter and Ravi Singh, "Marketing Warfare in the 1980s," *The Journal of Business Strategy,* Winter 1981.

13. Noel M. Tichy and David Ulrich, "The Challenge of Revitalization," *New Management,* Winter 1985, p. 54.

Chapter 4

1. Thomas Bonoma, *The Marketing Edge* (New York: The Free Press, 1985), p. 43.

2. Al Ries and Jack Trout, *Positioning: The Battle for Your Mind* (New York: Mcgraw-Hill, 1980), p. 11.

3. David Ogilvy, "Ogilvy on Advertising," *Advertising Age,* August 1, 1983, p. 52.

4. Buck Rodgers, *The IBM Way* (New York: Harper & Row, 1986), p. 125.

5. Ed Grimm, "Straight Talk," *Think,* 1987 (5), p. 9.

Chapter 5

1. "Business Executives Receive an Average of 44 Unsolicited Mail Pieces Each Week," *DM News,* July 15, 1985, p. 10.

2. Bob Stone, *Successful Direct Marketing Methods* (Lincolnwood, Ill.: Crain Books, 1987), p. 287.

3. Freeman Gosden, *Direct Marketing Success* (New York: John Wiley & Sons, 1985), p. 76.

4. Shell Alpert, "Spot the Creative Tiger by Its Stripes," *Business Marketing,* April 1989, p. 10.

5. Colin Wheildon, *Communicating, or Just Making Pretty Shapes?,* monograph, The Ogilvy Center for Research and Development, 1986.

6. Dick Hodgson, "Short Takes," *Direct,* April 20, 1989, p. 74.

Chapter 6

1. John Naisbitt, *Megatrends* (New York: Warner Books, 1984), p. 217.

2. Howard Aldrich, Ben Rosen, and William Woodward, "Social Behavior and Entrepreneurial Networks," in *Frontiers of Entrepreneurial Research* (Babson Park, Mass.: Babson College, 1986), pp. 239–240.

3. Leif Smith and Patricia Wagner, *The Networking Game* (Denver: Network Resources, 1981), p. 2.

4. Anne Boe and Bettie Youngs, *Is Your Net Working?* (New York: John Wiley & Sons, 1989), p. 50.

5. Robert R. Mueller, *Corporate Networking* (New York: The Free Press, 1986), p. 21.

6. Ibid., p. 19.

7. Ibid., p. 30.

8. Regis McKenna, *The Regis Touch* (New York: Addison Wesley, 1985), p. 57.

9. Robert Weisman, "Can't Afford a Consultant? Join the Club," *Wall Street Journal,* July 11, 1988, p. 18.

10. Sandra Sugawara, "Executives Lend a Helping Hand to Charities," *Washington Post,* December 26, 1988, p. 19.

11. McKenna, p. 16.

12. Sugawara, p. 19.
13. Pat Wagner and Leif Smith, *Manual for Using the Office for Open Network* (Denver: Network Resources, 1984), p. 28.

Chapter 7

1. Ray Bertrand, "Crafting 'Win-Win' Situations in a Buyer-Supplier Relationship," *Business Marketing*, June 1986, p. 50.
2. Warren Anderson, "The New Entrepreneurs," speech at the 1977 NAMA Conference.
3. Howard Sutton, "Keeping Tabs on the Competition," *Marketing Communications Magazine*, January 15, 1989, p. 42.
4. Buck Brown, "Enterprise," *Wall Street Journal*, June 29, 1989, p. B1.
5. Frank James, "If You Thought Nintendo Was Just a Game, You Lose," *Wall Street Journal*, June 6, 1989, p. B1.
6. John R. Wilke, "Down Time: At Digital Equipment Slowdown Reflects Industry's Big Changes," *Wall Street Journal*, September 15, 1989, p. A1.
7. Barbara Bund Jackson, "Build Customer Relationships That Last," *Harvard Business Review*, 1985, p. 124.
8. Jerry Bowles, "Focusing on the Customer," *Fortune*, June 1989, p. 218.
9. Theodore Levitt, *The Marketing Imagination* (New York: The Free Press, 1986), p. 124.
10. "IBM Offers Reassurances as Customers' Profits Dip, but It Concedes More Risks," *Wall Street Journal*, March 24, 1989, p. C1.
11. John A. Anderluh, from an address given at the National Account Marketing Association, Midwest Chapter, March 21, 1986.
12. Benson Shapiro, "Manage the Customer Not Just the Sales Force," *Harvard Business Review*, 1974, p. 128.
13. Buck Rodgers, *The IBM Way* (New York: Harper & Row, 1986), p. 143.

Chapter 8

1. Thomas Bonoma, "Major Sales: Who Really Does the Buying?" *Harvard Business Review*, May–June 1982.
2. Theodore Levitt, *The Marketing Imagination* (New York: The Free Press, 1986), p. 115.

Chapter 9

1. David Peoples, *Presentations Plus* (New York: John Wiley & Sons, 1988), p. 88.

2. "When You Tell the Boss, Plain Talk Counts," *Wall Street Journal*, June 16, 1989, p. B1.

3. D. Sears and J. Freedman, "Effects of Expected Familiarity with Arguments upon Opinion Change and Selective Exposure," *Journal of Personality and Social Psychology*, 1985, pp. 420–426.

4. Robert Cialdini, "Persuasion Principles," *Public Relations Journal*, October 1985, p. 12.

5. H. B. Gerard, "Conformity and Commitment to the Group," *Journal of Abnormal and Social Psychology*, 1964, pp. 209–211.

6. Donald J. Moine and John H. Herd, *Modern Persuasion Strategies* (Englewood Cliffs, N.J.: Prentice Hall, 1984), p. 44.

7. Lynn Oppenheim, Christine Kydd, Vincent P. Carroll, and Gregory Carroll, "A Study of the Effects of the Use of Overhead Transparencies on Business Meetings," Wharton Center for Applied Research and the Office of Education Services and Research School of Medicine, University of Pennsylvania, Philadelphia, 1981. Unpublished paper.

8. "Illustrations in Advertising Play a Significant Role in Leading a Reader/Prospect Up the Five Steps to a Sale," Report No. 5, McGraw-Hill Research, Laboratory of Advertising Performance, No. 3170.1, p. 3.

9. Anthony Jay, *Effective Presentation* (London: British Institute of Management Foundation, 1970), p. 50.

10. Moine and Herd, p. 93.

11. David Ogilvy, "Ogilvy on Advertising," *Advertising Age*, August 1, 1983, p. 52.

12. David Nadziejka, "Can They Read When You Speak?" *Bulletin of the American Society for Information Science*, January 1987, p. 22.

13. Miles Tinker and Donald Paterson, *How to Make Type Readable* (New York: Harper and Brothers, 1940), p. 209.

14. Colin Wheildon, *Communicating, or Just Making Pretty Shapes?*, monograph, The Ogilvy Center for Research and Development, 1986, pp. 20–21.

15. I. Janis, D. Kaye, and D. Kirschner, "Facilitating Effects of 'Eating-While-Reading' on Responsiveness to Persuasive Communications," *Journal of Personality and Social Psychology*, 1965 (1), pp. 181–186.

16. W. A. Watts and W. J. McGuire, "Persistence of Induced Opinion Change and Retention of the Inducing Message Contents," *Journal of Abnormal and Social Psychology*, 1964, pp. 223–241.

Chapter 10

1. Quoted in Ralph G. Nichols, "Listening Is Good Business," paper prepared for the Bureau of Industrial Relations (Ann Arbor: The University of Michigan, n.d.), p. 1.

2. Lyman K. Steil, Larry L. Barker, and Kittie W. Watsow, *Effective Listening: Key to Your Success* (New York: Addison-Wesley, 1983), p. 15.

3. Ron Winslow, "Sometimes, Talk Is the Best Medicine," *Wall Street Journal,* October 5, 1989, p. B1.

4. Ralph G. Nichols and Leonard A. Stevens, "Listening to People," *Harvard Business Review,* September–October 1957, p. 85.

5. Nichols, p. 3.

6. Ibid., pp. 4–8. The discussion that follows is based on concepts presented in Nichols's paper.

7. Nichols and Stevens, p. 57.

8. Edward de Bono, *Six Thinking Hats* (Boston: Little, Brown and Company, 1985), p. 52.

9. Ibid., p. 75.

10. Ibid., p. 108.

11. Ibid., p. 133.

12. Ibid., p. 135.

13. Ibid., p. 170.

14. Michael B. McCaskey, "The Hidden Messages Managers Send," *Harvard Business Review,* November–December 1979, p. 146.

15. Steil, Barker, and Watsow, p. 32.

16. McCaskey, p. 144.

17. Ibid.

18. Albert Mehrabian, "Communication Without Words," *Psychology Today,* September 1968, p. 54.

19. Amelia Lobsenz, "When a Nod Means No," *Public Relations Journal,* October 1987, p. 36.

20. Joseph H. Singer, "How to Work with Foreign Clients," *Public Relations Journal,* October 1987, p. 36.

21. Letitia Baldrige, *Complete Guide to Executive Manners* (New York: Rawson Associates, 1985), p. 183.

22. Carol J. Foulke, "Sensitivity to Cultures Builds Foreign Markets," *Marketing News,* June 19, 1989, p. 8.

23. John Fielden, "Communication—Meaning Is Shaped by Audience and Situation," *Personnel Journal,* May 1988, p. 108.

24. Joan E. Hoffman, "Want to Scare Away Business? Try 'CAP,' 'ATM,' 'Rollover,'" *Bottomline,* April 1985, p. 40.

25. Gary F. Soldow and Gloria Penn Thomas, "Relational Communication: Form Versus Content in the Sales Interaction," *Journal of Marketing,* Winter 1984, p. 85.

26. Mehrabian, p. 17.

Chapter 11

1. Bro Uttal, "Companies That Serve You Best," *Fortune,* December 1987, p. 98.

2. The Forum Corporation, "Customer Focus Research," *Executive Briefing,* April 1988, pp. 3–4.

3. Leonard Berry, "The Costs of Poor Quality Service Are Higher Than You Think," *American Banker,* June 24, 1987, p. 4.

4. The PIMS Data Base, "PIMS LETTER," No. 33, p. 8.

5. Karl Albrecht, *At America's Service* (Chicago: Dow Jones-Irwin, 1988), p. 69.

6. Ibid., p. 17.

7. Theodore Levitt, *The Marketing Imagination* (New York: The Free Press, 1986), p. 78.

8. Ibid., p. 84.

9. Leonard Berry, A. Parasuraman, and Valerie Zeithaml, "The Service-Quality Puzzle," *Business Horizons,* September–October 1988, pp. 35–41.

10. Tom Peters and Nancy Austin, *A Passion for Excellence* (New York: Random House, 1985), p. 76.

11. Albrecht, p. 26.

12. John Brooks, *Telephone: The First One Hundred Years* (New York: Harper & Row, Publishers, 1976), p. 345.

13. Alecia Swasy, "Slow and Steady," *Wall Street Journal,* September 21, 1989, p. A1.

14. Berry, Parasuraman, and Zeithaml, p. 37.

15. Tom Peters, *Thriving on Chaos* (New York: Alfred A. Knopf, 1987), p. 91.

16. "Increasing Consumer Satisfaction," United States Office of Consumers Affairs, in cooperation with Chevrolet Motor Division of General Motors, p. 4.

17. Ibid., p. 11.

18. Brent Bowers and Damon Darlin, "New Battleground: How Hotels in Japan and the United States Compare in the Services Game," *Wall Street Journal,* Sept. 21, 1988, p. 1.

19. Harry Bacas, "Making It Right for the Customer," *Nation's Business,* November 1987, p. 49.

20. Peters and Austin, p. 87.

21. "Increasing Consumer Satisfaction," p. 11.

22. Francine Schwadel, "Courting Shoppers," *Wall Street Journal,* August 1, 1989, p. A1.

23. Leonard Berry, David Bennett, and Carter Brown, *Service Quality* (Homewood, Ill.: Dow Jones-Irwin, 1989), p. 144.

Chapter 12

1. Harry J. Lew, "CIGNA Exec Says Cross-Selling Bears Fruit," *National Underwriter,* September 5, 1988, p. 12.

2. Brad Champlin, "Marketing Solutions: A Savings & Loan Hits Home," *Adweek's Marketing Week,* June 6, 1988, p. 50.

3. Jan L. Davis and Jonathan Cohn, "Marketing Financial Services in a Fragmented Market," *Bank Marketing,* January 1989, p. 25.

4. Harry J. Lew, "Cross Sales Start with Info Massage," *National Underwriter,* August 22, 1988, p. 17.

5. Lew, "CIGNA Executive Says Cross-Selling Bears Fruit," p. 12.

Chapter 13

1. Warren Bennis and Burt Nanus, *Leaders: The Strategies for Taking Charge* (New York: Harper & Row, 1985), p. 21.

2. Thomas Watson, Jr., *A Business and Its Beliefs* (New York: McGraw-Hill, 1963), p. 72.

3. Roger Smith, "The U.S. Must Do as GM Has Done," *Fortune,* February 13, 1989, p. 71.

4. Lawrence Schein, "A Manager's Guide to Corporate Culture," Report No. 926 (New York: The Conference Board, 1989), p. 1.

5. Julie Amparano Lopez, "Bucking Tradition: For the Baby Bells, New Business Ventures Beget a Culture Clash," *Wall Street Journal,* March 15, 1989, p. 1.

6. Andrew S. Grove, "My Turn: Breaking the Chains of Command," *Newsweek,* October 3, 1983, p. 23.

7. Robert E. Lefton and V. R. Buzzotta, "Teams That Work: A Study of Executive Level Teams," *National Productivity Review,* Winter 1987–1988, pp. 7–19.

8. Stanley J. Modic, "Grapevine Rated Most Believable," *Industry Week,* May 15, 1989, p. 11.

9. Lopez, p. 1.

10. Bennis and Nanus, p. 43.

11. Bob E. Wooten, "Organizational Communication: The Channel vs. the Grapevine," *Management World,* March 1981, pp. 39–40.

12. Ibid.

13. Watson, p. 55.

14. John Kotter, *The Leadership Factor* (New York: The Free Press, 1988), p. 87.

15. James M. Gustafson and Elmer W. Johnson, "Efficiency, Morality, and Managerial Effectiveness," in John R. Meyer and James M. Gustafson, eds., *The U.S. Business Corporation: An Institution in Transition* (Cambridge, Mass.: Ballinger, 1988), pp. 199–200.

16. "We Love You: More Companies Reward Workers Who Go That Extra Mile," *Wall Street Journal,* May 2, 1989, p. B1.

Index